LOVE + HATE

Hanif Kureishi grew up in Kent and studied philosophy at King's College London. His novels include *The Buddha of Suburbia*, which won the Whitbread Prize for Best First Novel, *The Black Album*, *Intimacy* and *The Last Word*. His screenplays include *My Beautiful Laundrette*, which received an Oscar nomination for Best Screenplay, *Sammy and Rosie Get Laid* and *Le Week-End*. He has also published several collections of short stories. He has been awarded the Chevalier de l'Ordre des Arts et des Lettres, the PEN/Pinter Prize and is a Commander of the Order of the British Empire. His work has been translated into thirty-six languages. He is professor of Creative Writing at Kingston University.

by the same author

LOVE + HATE
Stories and Essays

HANIF KUREISHI

FABER & FABER

First published in 2015
by Faber and Faber Limited
Bloomsbury House
74–77 Great Russell Street
London WC1B 3DA
This paperback edition published in 2016

Typeset by Faber and Faber Limited
Printed in the UK by CPI Group (UK) Ltd, Croydon, CR0 4YY

A CIP record for this book
is available from the British Library

ISBN 978-0-571-31970-1

FSC
www.fsc.org
MIX
Paper from
responsible sources
FSC® C101712

2 4 6 8 10 9 7 5 3 1

to Sachin Kureishi

Contents

Flight 423

The stewardess brought Daniel a glass of champagne and some roasted nuts. The champagne wasn't good, but it would lighten his heavy head and reduce his irritability. Standing, he drank it back at once and was relieved to hand his jacket to the smiling stewardess and remove his shoes, settling into his seat not long before the plane was due to leave the gate. He was aware that people with real money went private. Still, you didn't get this service on a bus. He would enjoy a temporary, restful passivity. It had taken him years to reach this condition of ease; he'd make the most of it – particularly after what he'd just endured.

He had been late getting to the airport from his hotel. He travelled often, and it had become his habit, on the flight home, to loiter with several drinks, food and the newspapers in the aimless area of the First Class Lounge. But he'd been stuck in a terrible meeting, his driver was delayed and the road to the airport was blocked. Airport security – or 'insecurity', as his teenage children called it – had been obtrusive and slow. Although he always checked the news at least twice an hour, he wondered if there'd been an incident he hadn't heard about. In the security hall – a sweaty shed of crawling conveyor belts carrying luggage, clothes and shoes past monitors – he'd had to watch strangers undress, before removing his own clothes, apart from trousers and T-shirt. He was made to stand inside an X-ray machine so security personnel could inspect his organs, for fear he was concealing toxic material in his heart or kidneys.

At last he could relax. Soon he would eat. There'd be more to drink. He'd watch a movie, but he had to sleep. To be certain, he'd brought his pills. At the end of the working day, two hours after the seven-hour flight landed in his home city, he was due at a meeting which at least ten people would attend. He'd need to check his notes and prepare himself. He was keen to feel fresh. There would be a driver at the airport holding up a sign with his name on it. He hoped the car was quiet, with darkened windows. He would sink into himself, wearing headphones to block out the street noise. If his latest documentary project was green-lit, he and his company could survive another two years. Otherwise he might have to close it, lay off the employees and find something else to do, if, indeed, there was anything out there. In his mid-fifties, he could be facing a long idleness. Many of his friends were beginning to slow down, moving to the country and working less, but his situation could never be as comfortable.

At the gate he'd been informed that the flight would

be packed. When he boarded, before turning to the front of the plane, he'd glanced into the economy section and seen that, sure enough, all the seats appeared to be taken. Gazing at the rows of faces, he felt a surge of claustrophobia: hundreds of strangers forced together – unwittingly smelling, touching and looking at one another – as they sat in a narrow pipe flung through the air at fantastic speed. Why would he worry? He'd flown hundreds of times; it was no different to travelling on the subway and, on arrival, he'd never think of it again.

The place he'd booked was in the second row. His section of the plane was more sedate, but it wasn't paradise. In the seat ahead of him sat a young woman feeding a baby. Across the aisle was a man in his early thirties reading the newspaper, presumably the child's father. At present the baby was chuckling and gurgling. With two children himself, Daniel was aware how rapidly moods could switch in a child.

The air stewardess refilled his glass. To his left sat a smart woman in her early forties. Wearing black, she had expensive hair: tinted, streaked and highlighted. At her feet was a box. He watched as she opened it and pulled out a wrinkly faced, snub-nosed dog which sneezed and looked at him. He was surprised and a little agitated. He'd never seen a dog on a plane before. Was it allowed? Suppose it barked and tried to bite him? Suppose the animal shat?

3

He glanced at other passengers to see whether they'd noticed. Behind the dog woman was a slim but wide-chested, possibly Spanish or Italian man in sports clothes, with a baseball cap pulled down over his forehead and white headphone buds in his ears, looking like someone who didn't want to be recognised. Daniel stared hard and could make him out: he was a well-known footballer. Daniel was pleased; he'd be able to impress his kids and their friends if, when the man was asleep, he got a photograph.

The dog woman now had the animal on her lap and appeared to be talking to it. When the stewardess passed Daniel, he indicated the dog, but she only shrugged and brought him another drink. If there was anything she could get him, he just had to ask.

The child screamed throughout the flight and the father refused to meet Daniel's glare of reproach. The dog slept on the woman's chest and didn't bark or shit. The stewardess and her colleagues pushed a trolley through the cabin containing watches, pens, electronic goods and perfumes. They were forgettable fool's trinkets; he thought of his basement at home, full of discarded things that had cost money. And he was broke, by which he meant that he spent all he earned. But the alcohol made him intelligently reckless. Money came and went; he worried and counted it and fantasised about having more of it, yet nothing much changed. He liked to say that he was secure, yet insecure, like the world.

He considered taking something home for the kids and his wife but fell asleep. Hours later, as they approached the city, he began to gather his books and papers. They were told there would be a fifteen-minute delay due to congestion.

This Daniel had anticipated; he'd made sure his assistant had left time for him to get to the meeting. He hoped it wouldn't take long for him to pick up his luggage and clear the airport. However, after thirty minutes they were informed there'd be a further delay. They were in a stack and would have to circle the city. He was impatient, yet had to admit the city looked exquisite as they circled: imperious, wealthy and cultured with its banks, churches, galleries and parks, and the glittering diamond-studded snake of the river lying across it. He loved that view, but not so much he wanted to see it four times.

Forty minutes later another announcement: it wasn't good news. There had been a computer blackout on the ground and planes were unable to land for the time being. A groan went around. People sighed and cursed and drummed their feet. Daniel asked the stewardess how long 'the time being' was, receiving a shrug in reply.

As they looped the city he could see it darkening. *His* air stewardess brought him more drinks, and he didn't like to refuse for fear it would encourage her to be negative. She told him her name, Bridget, and brought another drink. He couldn't tell how intoxicated he was, but it wasn't enough. He warned himself to be careful. They could still be off this plane in thirty minutes and he had a meeting to attend that would decide important matters. But there was something about being in the impersonal space of an aircraft, like a hotel or a hospital, that could make one irresponsible, if not overexcited.

After one more tour of the city, the seatbelt sign came on and the captain told passengers to return to their seats. Standing passengers hurried as the plane dipped and trembled in the wind. This turbulence made Daniel buoyant. They must have entered another fresh patch of sky. They were descending and all would be fine. He drank some water and shook his head to clear it.

Following another announcement about the 'ongoing' delay, Bridget came over to tell him that the malfunction wasn't quite repaired. And when it was, it would be a while before they got down since scores of flights ahead of them had been circling for hours.

Time passed and other passengers fretted and protested as they missed connections and appointments. He missed his meeting; it would be clear to those waiting how and why. He was not even annoyed now and was able to stop composing angry letters of complaint. How little time, in the actual world, did he put aside for contemplation. So he contemplated: he became moved by his own helplessness, and wept a little at the thought of his children doing their homework at the kitchen table or in their rooms, and his wife of three years telling her step-children not to worry, their father would be back soon. It was important he saw the kids. They'd go to school in the morning; it would be another two weeks before they came again. And loved, at last, he longed for his wife's frequent kisses; it occurred to him that the loved and the unloved are a different species.

There was a further announcement, this time from the reassuring voice of the captain. Engineers were busy working on the malfunction, which had closed many airports. Passengers were not to worry, the work was proceeding successfully. It would be about ninety minutes before they landed, and meanwhile passengers were encouraged to relax, enjoy the rest of their flight and choose this airline again.

Bridget fetched Daniel a Bloody Mary and, answering his question, laughed and said she had no idea whether it had been a terrorist cyber-attack or not, but she thought it unlikely. Daniel sat through another movie and thought of his friends having supper; he imagined their houses, their talk, their food and their ignorance of the futility he was experiencing. To prevent himself becoming too maudlin, he took another pill, watched the city grow dim and the lights come on, turned over and tried to sleep. When he awoke, they'd be on the ground and he'd go straight home. The meeting would be rearranged. The world was hell itself, but most misfortunes happened to other people.

It was dark when he woke up at three thirty in the morning, parched, hungry and aching. Despite being at the luxury end of the plane, he felt as though he'd slept on a park bench, and crucifixion would have been preferable. Some passengers were moving about the plane but the staff were absent – asleep, he guessed. He drank some water. This was the longest air delay he'd experienced.

He must have dropped off again, because the next thing he was aware of was some sort of commotion. 'Hey, what d'you think you're doing?' someone said. There were other raised voices behind him, and peals of agreement. 'Stop him, stop him,' said someone else. 'Call the captain!' What was the man doing?

Daniel turned to look and then rose to get closer.

There was no actual resistance to the uprising which appeared to be going on. A huge man with a large head whom Daniel had noticed earlier at the back of the plane had left his place. His torso barely concealed by a sweat-stained T-shirt, and weakly supported on his little legs, the man had abandoned his seat in the centre of a row and was determinedly moving along the aisle, clutching each headrest as he went, before butting through the curtain and into the segregated area of Business Class. He collapsed into the empty seat behind the footballer, snatched at the control which converted the seat into a bed, rolled over and fell asleep noisily.

The passengers in Daniel's section – apart from the footballer, who looked at no one – caught one another's eyes. Daniel looked away: he'd realised that what was horrible was the idea that these formerly anonymous people could become real, and might even begin to matter to him a little. He would have to forfeit his superiority, even his contempt, in exchange for sympathetic exchange with strangers.

'Well, well,' he said, looking at the snoring huge man. Without the assistance of the rugged midfielder, who would attempt to move or dispute with him? Who had the authority or will? Bridget and her other colleagues, who had appeared at the scene, merely stood and watched, before returning to the galley. Daniel went back to his seat and stared ahead. It was a turning point: the barricades had been stormed, the Berlin Wall had been breached and nothing would be the same in this prison in the sky. 'Oh God,' he said. 'Who will help us!'

'No one!' said the dog woman. 'No one cares! We have been forgotten.'

'I doubt it,' said Daniel. 'How could you forget an airplane?'

Bridget leaned over him and said, 'If you can, get some sleep. We're going to be up here for a while. It's proving difficult to find out what's going on.'

As she spoke he touched her arm, and she didn't move hers. Since he had married for a second time he'd been faithful to his lover, friend and wife as he'd promised he would. But here, perhaps he could make an exception. He laughed to himself: how foolish all this was making them.

He drank a couple of beers, Bridget covered him up and tucked him in, and he managed to pass out. But eventually, despite his efforts, he had no choice but to wake up. Consciousness was no longer a blessing. Then there was more day, and everything in front of him had shifted.

The galley was crowded with passengers from the back of the plane, who were hunched and concentrated. The area resembled the back door of Daniel's local supermarket, where beggars would gather around the bins to collect unwanted food. The passengers riffled through drawers and cupboards, pulled out bread rolls, grabbed water bottles, scuffled over fruit and secured whatever food they could grab inside their clothes. He was hungry himself, he realised, but he wasn't ready yet to fight for an apple.

Daniel opened the blind next to him and saw they were flying higher than before and, possibly, still in a circle. In the distance he glimpsed three other planes but he couldn't see the ground. It was bright daylight, and even colder in the plane now. His mouth stank of burnt things; his stomach was empty. He found beside him a full bottle of water, which he sipped from surreptitiously and then concealed, for fear someone would see.

He had held on for as long as he could, but it was time for him to go to the toilet again. He attempted to walk to the back of the plane to stretch his legs and see what conditions were like. It took him some time; he tried to step carefully. There were heads, hands and feet scattered everywhere, as if someone had flung them on the floor. People were sleeping in the aisles, freeing space for others to lie on the seats. Daniel tripped and fell into someone who punched him in the side; as he tried to get up, they socked him again. 'Hey!' he shouted. 'Look out – I'm a person!' It was a refugee scene of some despair, a barely living pile of humanity, noisy with groans and complaints. People asked him for food as he passed. Someone lit a cigarette. The ceiling appeared to be dripping but he didn't understand why.

He was surprised, when he got to the rear of what had become a flying slum, to see that a restroom was free and the door ajar. Pushing it open he realised the toilet was overflowing with excrement. There was even faeces on the walls. He retched, covered his face with his sweater and zigzagged back to Business.

They had been in the plane at least eighteen hours more than expected. Bridget was sitting on her little seat with her head in her hands. The dog woman had covered her head with a blanket, the dog was coughing and whimpering at her feet, and the footballer, who had not removed his cap, sat with his mouth open, unblinking, staring ahead of him. The couple with the baby were asleep. The toilet in the Business section was not unlike the toilet at the other end of the plane. He recalled someone telling him that the measure of a civilisation was how it disposed of its excrement. He held his nose, pulled down his pants and shat on the floor like everyone else, wiping his arse on the in-flight magazine, something he'd always dreamed of doing, and flinging the paper into the rest of the mess.

He found a bottle of perfume on the floor. The gift trolley had been raided. There was nothing left: empty boxes were strewn about, and Daniel, following the example of another passenger, took the wise decision to douse himself in scent.

He rolled up his trouser legs and was rubbing something called Glory into his calves, when the footballer rose up and padded towards the toilet. He had Daniel's initial reaction, raising and lowering his cap in concern, before sharply turning his head away in revulsion. Watching this it occurred to Daniel what difficulty they must be in if the footballer's club had left someone like him hanging in the air. That piece of meat was worth many millions of pounds, far more than everyone else on the flight put together.

He stood in the galley, where Bridget was leaning against the counter with her colleagues. Her work smile was gone, her face was pinched and her lips dry. No one here would seek out their own reflection.

She had never experienced anything like this and was intending to retire when they got back. The air had become too dangerous. Not that they were unsafe exactly. The plane had been refuelled during the night; the authorities couldn't have it just drop out of the sky into the city or sea. She guessed the reason they weren't able to use another airport or land in another country was because the computer virus had spread. Perhaps somewhere a plane had already crashed on landing, rendering the runway inoperable. However, Bridget hadn't lost her habit of reassurance: there was no doubt they would land the next day when normal service had been resumed.

'How do you know?' he asked.

'It must be true,' she said. 'Surely? If they can make a computer, they must be able to fix it.'

She said she had acquired something for him. Checking that no one would oversee, she passed him a roll wrapped in cling film. It was the last one 'ever'. After this they would have to 'diet'. He hadn't eaten meat in twenty years, but he smiled and thanked her for the tiny stale ham roll. It was that or nothing.

As he chewed, even as the taste rose in his throat, he noticed an old woman from the back of the plane wobbling up the aisle. He supposed she wanted to use the toilet, but she stopped at his seat, repositioned and plumped his cushion and then flapped his scratchy blanket. She was about to sit in his seat. The Business section was full, other passengers, following the huge man's revolt, having come up from the rear of the plane.

He hurried to his place, slipping in sideways under her arm just before she could sit down, whispering, 'So sorry, but I have a bad back,' as she attacked him in a language he couldn't understand. He didn't dare look at the disappointed woman for fear he would be shamed, but instead stared miserably out of the window until she stopped begging him. This seat, he thought, is the last thing I have and I'm staying here.

He leaned over towards the woman with the little dog. She was muttering, 'Find me, find me, find me,' and he gave her a small part of the roll, which she pushed into the gobbling mouth of the dog. 'Thank you.'

Night came for the second time. Daniel walked a little, but never went beyond the area of his seat for fear that someone would steal it. The law, or even decency, no longer applied in this exceptional zone. He urinated in empty water bottles and rolled them behind his seat; he shat in sick bags and tossed them into the toilet. Excrement and urine were seeping down the aisles; the air was fetid, breathing an agony. He yearned for a breeze. He was surprised by how quickly things had deteriorated, and what a thin membrane it was that kept civilisation and hell apart.

Time passed as it does, until in the middle of the night there was some interest when the captain, flanked by a haggard steward for security, left his cockpit once more to stretch his legs and attempt some yoga positions. Both his and the steward's uniforms were filthy. At the start of this catastrophe, the passengers had looked to the pilot with hope and expectation, considering him to have special knowledge of how things worked up here. He murmured a few words. 'We're working on it. We're trying our damned best – you can be sure everyone in the company is working day and night to get us out of here. As it is, we're perfectly safe, if a little uncomfortable. Please stay in your seats, be patient and we'll get you down.'

At the sight of him, the passengers had hastened to the front in a crowd to hear. But when they saw the captain's ashen face they didn't listen for a minute before yelling, 'You know nothing, you asshole. Why are you lying? You're a disgusting idiot, a total fool, scum,' and so on, until he scuttled back to his cabin and locked the door.

Since the captain had little to say, many realistic and fantastical explanations went round the plane. The city had broken down irrevocably, its cyber-system destroyed and thousands of people killed; the plane been 'kidnapped' by terrorists and the passengers were being used in secret negotiations – some of them would be exchanged for prisoners from elsewhere; the Earth had been partly destroyed by an asteroid. Their lot was 'fate', he heard often; it was 'God's will' was the most tiresome of all. He thought, What a lot of jabber tragedy provides an excuse for. His view – that they were hanging from the spittle of a giant lizard – would not have been popular.

Many thought they were done for. They had flown through a storm; the plane had been flung about in the void; lightning flashed around them. Daniel was sick several times, though there was nothing in his stomach. He had no idea how the other passengers were able to make such terrible noises. People called out, 'Please shut up!' but it made no difference.

He was lying semi-comatose, neither asleep nor awake, when he heard other noises. Getting to his feet he saw that a blanket had been pinned up around the footballer's seat. The footballer was the one person on the plane who didn't complain or speak, but now he was copulating. Daniel moved enough to see that it was Bridget he was copulating with. Their pushing and thrashing brought down the blanket, and Daniel saw Bridget's breasts were exposed and the man had pulled his trousers down to his knees. What a story this would be for the kids when Daniel got home.

Bridget got up and returned to the galley. Daniel closed his eyes but the footballer was standing over him. 'Hey,' he said. 'Were you watching me?'

'Watching what?' said Daniel.

'Don't do that again,' said the footballer. He reached out and took Daniel by the throat. 'Do you have any water?'

'I have just a little left.'

'Give it.'

Daniel found his bottle concealed under his seat cushion and gave it to the midfielder. The footballer finished the water, crushed the bottle and handed it back.

'If you come across any more, bring it to me.'

'Yes,' said Daniel, thinking, I won't be found at the bottom of the sea holding hands with you. It wasn't the right time to ask for a selfie.

He sat in his seat with a soiled blanket around him for some time, before venturing, cowed and hunched, into the galley, where he was surprised to discover that he now had the aspect of a street beggar. 'Please, Bridget, is there anything else to eat? That's all I need to know. You can tell me. Please whisper. Have you found anything at all?'

She shook her head. 'Up here we're out of everything, including water. But we should be down soon.'

'How do you know?' he asked.

'I feel it,' she said.

'Thank you,' he said, adding, 'Don't forget me if you find anything.'

As they continued the infinite repetition for hours in the darkness there were many hubbubs, howlings and disputes, over things like the little alcohol that was left, apples, and whose turn it was to lie on the floor and who could attempt to exercise in the restricted space. There was even a vicious fight when a woman grabbed the hair of another woman and tried to smash her face into the fuselage. Daniel had wondered whether someone should attempt to introduce some civility or even democracy into this non-space and non-time. Nevertheless, apart from the morose footballer, everyone did address everyone else, and there was a minimal element of organisation. A couple from the back of the plane brought food for the baby – and so did others – which the parents accepted gratefully, as the woman had stood up several times to scream, 'My child will die – he'll die!'

The despair and lassitude was general – the dog was curled up in the dog woman's footrest, completely still; the footballer removed his cap to bang his forehead repeatedly on the back of the seat in front of him – but anything involving the huge man was dramatic. If he had appeared cussed at the start of the trip, by now he was impossible. He had been telling everyone around him that the situation was 'too much' and he had 'had enough'. This would have crossed the minds of many people on the flight. If the world had somehow disappeared, while they were eternal, suicide was a nice thought to have in the circumstances.

It was nearly morning when the huge man stabbed himself in the chest with a cutlery knife and didn't make an entirely triumphant job of it: the knife needed to go several more inches into the body. Joining the crowd around the man, Daniel saw him sitting there with his mouth open and the erect blade sticking out of him. It would take some time, but he would bleed to death. At that moment the huge man was attempting to get to his feet and – even in his condition – began to stagger towards the back of the plane, declaring, 'I'm getting out of here.'

'Good luck!' someone shouted. 'Shut the door behind you!'

'Hold the door!' yelled someone else. 'I'm coming too!'

As he turned away from the man, Daniel stumbled and almost collapsed into the detritus on the floor. He had become so used to the calm trajectory of the unanchored, ever-turning plane that he was surprised to feel it roll and rise. He sat down and opened the blind. It was early afternoon and they seemed to be heading into the city again. The engines accelerated. Surely they would land soon. They had suffered, but all would be well; he would run from the plane and walk on the earth again. He would be glad to see everyone; they might even be relieved to see him. What a lesson in love this had been.

The plane banked, and rose. It seemed to have intention now. There was a moment of blinding sunlight, and he covered his eyes. When it straightened and he looked down again, he saw the suburbs with a motorway running through them; the traffic was moving smoothly. The plane followed this road until Daniel could see fields. It wasn't long before they reached the coast. Briefly there was a beach with what looked like insects crossing it, and soon they were heading out to sea.

They were moving away from the Earth. He thought he understood it now. There was some disorder in the world they had to leave behind. As something appeared to be happening and he felt he was sitting with his feet in damp mould, he decided it was time to put his shoes on. He would be prepared. Turning one shoe over, he found a small stone within the corrugation of the sole. He extracted it and weighed it, looking at it in the open cup of his hand. It was round like the earth and smooth as a pearl.

Anarchy and the Imagination

Ever since I was a teenager I've collected 'How to' books about writing. I have a shelf of them, and recently I was looking at some material about plot, structure and narrative, the technical part of writing, thinking I might pick up something new. There are courses about this stuff everywhere all the time, and, as writing teachers, there are questions we are asked constantly: about the 'arc' and the 'journey', or 'How do you make the structure work?' 'What is good dialogue?' These are boring questions, and the answers are boring. The teacher and the student are enacting their roles perfectly, keeping everything nicely mundane, only talking about things which can be taught, or maybe learned. Through being mortified like this, the whole question of art then seems manageable, though. But obviously the most important element is missing.

If you think of the real thing – of, say, Mary Shelley's *Frankenstein*, or Stevenson's *Jekyll and Hyde*, or Wilde's *Dorian Gray*, or perhaps Cheever's great story 'The Swimmer', or Kafka's 'The Metamorphosis', or any of the work of Carver or a poet, such as Plath – you have to begin to think about the wild implausibility, boldness and brilliance of the artist's idea or metaphor rather than the arrangement of paragraphs. Once you start thinking about this you have to think about the imagination and how it works, of where it might come from, and where it might take you. You're in useful trouble.

Most people have good ideas all the time, they just prefer not to notice them. Yet the authors just mentioned found solutions to conflicts which were bothering or even tormenting them, conflicts which must have seemed like holes or impossibilities at the time, and which eventually demanded a creative leap into a new way of seeing. Their imaginations were transformative, a going beyond, requiring that a new thing be made out of old things, which were then put together in shocking and disruptive combinations which are fresh even today.

It could easily be the case that unbearable conflict might produce depression or self-hatred. You could call depression 'a failure of the imagination', a self-sabotaging refusal to consider a creative solution or look forward. Such conflicts might also produce art, the work itself representing the 'impossibility'. In Franz Kafka's masterpiece 'The Metamorphosis', the protagonist, Gregor Samsa, wakes up one morning to find he has turned into a dung beetle. This illustrates, amongst many other things, Kafka's relation to his own family, showing an imaginative flight from his own personal impasse, and how an altruistic sacrifice might benefit the whole family. Kafka was thinking about the emergency of his life. He couldn't talk about it, and he couldn't *not* talk about it. He couldn't change his life, either; he was too masochistic for that; he just wrote. Being truly transgressive, when it comes to our own rules, is one of the most difficult things there is. However, Kafka's internal editor made him inventive; his crisis provoked a metaphor, and he wrote a story, putting the malady in the reader, so that it might change our lives. Kafka found a beautiful compromise – at least from the point of view of literary history.

Romantics such as Wordsworth and Coleridge knew that the imagination is as dangerous as dynamite, not only politically – the populace might have new, important, if dissident, ideas – but also inside an individual. The imagination can feel like disorder, when it is, in fact, an illumination. There is no doubt that the imagination *is* hazardous, and should be; there are certain thoughts which are combustible, and must be repressed or foreclosed. Good and evil, as in a bad film, must be kept separate. There are notions here which cannot be fully conceived of or thought, which must not be put together, which cannot fuse, develop or seem ambiguous. That is because like dreaming, the imagination can be antisocial. Plato would have banned art from his ideal state because it was fake, or 'an imitation', as he put it, and might overstimulate the populace. And we know, of course, that writers and artists throughout history have been attacked, censored and jailed, for having thoughts or ideas which other people cannot bear to hear. From this point of view, the Word is always risky. So it should be.

The imagination rarely behaves well. It can be ignored and censored, but never entirely willed away. Such a willing away would be a mistake because, unlike fantasy, which is inert and unchanging – in fantasy we tend to see the same things repeatedly – the imagination represents hope, rebirth and a new way of being. If fantasy is a return of the already-known and familiar, you might say that an inspiration is a suddenly uncovered part of the self, something newly seen or understood. Emerson, who tells us in 'Compensation' that 'growth comes by shocks', writes, in another essay, 'Nature', 'The best moments of life are these delicious awakenings of the higher powers.'

One of my students said he read books in order to have 'more ideas about life'. You'd have to say that the imagination is an essential faculty, and that it can be developed and followed. It is as necessary as love because without it we are trapped in the bleak polarities of either/or, in a North Korea of the mind, deadly and empty, with not much to look at. Without imagination we cannot reconceive what we know, or see far enough. The imagination, while struggling with inhibition, represents more thought and possibility; it is myriad, complex, liquid, wild and erotic. Art defamiliarises, and so does the imagination. The banal world seems strange again. It opens in new ways.

The imagination is not only an instrument of art. We cannot delegate speculation to artists. It isn't only artists who put difficult things together, make things up, and require and utilise vision. Whether we like it or not, we are all condemned to be artists. We are the creators and artists of our own lives, of the future and of the past – of whether, for instance, we view the past as a corpse, a resource, or something else. We are artists in the way we see, interpret and construct the world. We are daily artists, of play, conversation, walks, food, friendship, sex and love. Every kiss, every piece of work or meal, every exchanged word and every heard thing – there are better ways of listening – has some art in it, or none.

To survive successfully in the world requires huge capability. And to be bold and original is difficult labour; it can seem impossible, because we have histories and characters that can become fixed identities. We are made before we know it; we are held back by who we were made into. Not only that, we are inhabited by destructive, chattering devils who want less than the best for us. It is a struggle to live freely; identities become halted. Internalised, irrelevant versions of the law and custom limit us; there's nothing as dangerous as safety, keeping us from reinvention and recreation. Imaginative work can seem destructive, and might annihilate that to which we are most attached. Naturally, if we can do this, we pay for our pleasures in guilt. However, in the end, misery and despair are more expensive, and make us ill. Let madness be our guide, but not our destination.

Aspiring writers who wish to be taught plot, structure and narrative are not mistaken, but following rules doesn't make anyone an artist. The rules produce only obedience and mediocrity. The artist asks questions about moral authority itself. 'Structure', for the artist, *is* imagination.

Great writing and great ideas are strange: their sorcery and magic are more like dreaming with intent than descriptions of the world. Daily art makes and remakes the world, giving it meaning and substance. It's a responsibility. You could lose your voice, you could write 'I Am the Walrus', or you could throw a party. The imagination creates reality rather than imitates it. There is no interesting consensus about the way the world is. In the end, there is nothing out there but what we make of it, and whether we make more or less of it is a daily question about how we want to live and who we want to be.

The Racer

He and his wife had joked, for several years, about having a race around the streets where they lived. Now, in the week of their divorce, before they moved out of the house they'd shared with the children and stepchildren for twelve years, they would do it, neither of them having been able to find a reason to back down. It would, he guessed, be the last thing they did together.

He'd jogged twice a week for the past five years, but had rarely managed more than twenty minutes. And while she practised yoga and liked to dance the bossa nova, she took no other exercise. She had the racing edge, though, being in her mid-forties, while he was in his early sixties, which, he had discovered, was an uncomfortable age of earnest and critical self-reflection.

Compared to him, his rival wasn't in bad shape, but she couldn't be said to be in good shape. In her teenage years she had been a cross-country runner. She was built for it: tall but chubby, with strong, thick legs. She would be very determined, he knew that. Nonetheless, he didn't believe she had sufficient stamina. You couldn't just run for over an hour at a hard pace if you hadn't done it for twenty-five years. Or could you, if bitterness was your fuel? She had said, when they discussed it, that she could 'never, ever' let him beat her. She would rather kill herself. Let her die then, he thought. He'd bury her gladly.

Now the two of them strode out through the house to the pavement. The kids and their friends, excited and bewildered by the eccentric behaviour of the adults, banged at the windows and waved them off, before going back to playing football in the echoing rooms which were empty now, apart from packed boxes marked with his and hers stickers.

He was aware that none of them would forget this day, and he wasn't taking it lightly. For a start, he realised they had seriously underestimated the distance. Based on the course they had agreed, the whole race would probably take an hour and a half. This was, for them both, more than an effort.

Ever since they'd finally agreed to the 'death match', he had started to practise, running about thirty minutes most days, exhausted at the end. The previous evening he'd attempted ten press-ups, drunk little, worked out, and at nine thirty retired to his room, where he'd imagined himself, the next day, crashing into the house ahead of her, with his arms upraised like Jesse Owens in Berlin, but with a rose in his teeth.

Central to his hope was that fury would inspire and

carry him through, particularly after she'd said, 'Truly, I hope I get home first. Then I can call you an ambulance, and you can see me wave from the pavement, flat on your fucking back, you gutted loser.'

The kids, he noted, were keen to know what he'd put in his will.

Outside on the street, he bent forward and backwards, and jiggled on his toes, churning his arms. She stood next to him impatiently. He couldn't bear to look at her. She had said that she was eager to get on with her life. For that he was glad. Surely, then, he couldn't take this ridiculous bout seriously? The two of them must have looked idiotic, standing there glaring, seething and stamping. Where was his wisdom and maturity? Yet, somehow, nothing had been as important as this before.

He concentrated on his breathing and began to jog on the spot. He would run to the edge of himself. He would run because he'd made another mistake. He would run because they could not be in the same room, and because the worst of her was inside him.

When he thought she was ready, he said, 'All right?'

'Yes.'

'Let's start then. Are you sure?' he said.

'Yes, I'm sure.'

'Ready?'

She said, 'Say "go", not "ready".'

'I will. When you agree it's time to say it.'

'Just say it now, please,' she said. 'For God's sake!'

'Okay, okay.'

'Okay?' she said.

'Go!' he said.

'Right, thanks,' she said. 'At last. You made a decision.'

'Go, go!' he said.

'Good,' she said. 'Go!'

And they went.

He started first, taking a few careful paces to try his knees, only to see her hare off, flying past him, and turning the corner a few yards away. Soon she was out of sight.

He kept to his plan; he was slow, as he had intended, conserving his energy for the final fifteen-minute burst. Turning the first corner himself, he slowed down even more. He'd felt a tightening in his left calf. Something stringy must have pulled. Could it be multiple sclerosis? Or perhaps cramp? These days he even got cramp reaching to cut his toenails. Not that anyone was excused: you'd see them before extra time at football tournaments; on two hundred grand a week, the world's greatest footballers lying on the turf as if they'd been shot. He knew their agony; he shared it, this hopping devastated fool in luminous running shoes, with linen shorts over scraggy legs.

On he went towards the Green, believing he'd either run his twinges off or become accustomed to the pain. Much worse than this, he soon learned, was the public exposure, the panting parade of shame. Many pedestrians seemed to be walking faster than he ran, but he did get past a banker's au pair pushing a child. A Polish builder he knew was unloading his van, and the Hungarian waiters from his local cafe, on their way to work, were keen to smile and wave, and offer him a cigarette. His neighbours, a lawyer, a madman and a journalist, were easy to pass. The dry cleaner, contemplating eternity outside his shop, didn't see him.

He noticed couples who could abide one another all day, who would eat breakfast and talk together in holiday hotels, and felt like a man who'd opened a pornographic website only to see awful images of consummated happiness and joyful love-making among the married, more obscene than obscenity.

He ran past the private school, the state school and the French school, as well as the Chinese church, the Catholic church, and the mosque which occupied the ground floor of a house. He flew past Tesco's and several corner shops, as well as an Indian restaurant, a Moroccan coffee shop, and several charity shops. In the window of one, he saw a display of the books he didn't have room for in his small new flat where, he believed, the nights all lasted a hundred years. He would wake to no family sounds. He had to learn to live again. And why would anyone want to do that?

It was some relief to make it into the park, and to see other grimacing self-scourgers, many even older. This was where he spotted his rival again, the wife he couldn't love or kill. There she was, a tiny figure pumping strongly into the wind, across the far side of the grass. She disappeared through the trees, apparently untiring.

After a concentrated circuit of the park, he came out onto the pavement for a bit. Dodging the commuters, he headed down into a fetid underpass where his footsteps were loud, and up and out onto the towpath beside the vast surprise of the river. Public schoolboys and girls in wellington boots, with their lives ahead of them, pulled long boats out onto the water.

He skirted them and, after about fifteen minutes, came to the bridge. He looked up and ran half the steps. It would be wise, he thought, to plod the rest. He was breathing heavily, and coughing, being not a Cartesian vessel of higher consciousness and rationality, but rather a shapeless bag of bursting tendons, extruding veins and screaming lungs.

Yet some spark of agency remained, and on the bridge he jogged again, glimpsing the wide view, and the eyes of the lovely houses overlooking it, places he'd never afford now. Home is for children, he thought, tossing his wedding ring over the side. Perhaps there was a pile of the golden ones down there, just under the surface, the bitter debris of love, and a tribute to liberation.

Holding tight onto the handrail for fear of plunging down headfirst, he reached the bottom of the steps on the other side and turned, with a madly confident kick of speed, onto the street. After another hundred yards he took a breather. He had to.

It would be a lengthy final stretch now, along the avenue of loss, with the tree-lined river on one side and the reservoir on the other. Further along this path, if he didn't have a heart attack, he would find his wife collapsed and whimpering, or perhaps even vomiting, with only sufficient energy to claw at his ankles, pleading. Not that he'd stop. He'd leap over her, maybe giving her a little accidental kick in the head, before firing on to victory.

After slogging up and down those steps, he knew he was tiring, or else could die. He'd had enough of this run, and required all his reserve power. Where was it? He tied and retied his shoes and then ran on the spot, afraid of stopping, as he contemplated the wet vista of mud, trees and clouds ahead of him. And all the while his mind whirled and turned, counting his losses, until the search for suffering came to a stop. He'd had a better idea. He took a step.

Instead of following her, instead of perhaps catching up with her at last, he turned and faced the other way. He took another step. He took several steps, a little off balance, as if he'd never walked before. He was away. Going in the other direction.

Like Zeno's arrow, shot through the air forever, he would never get there. He would get somewhere else.

Weren't there other places but here? He would be a missing person. Sometimes you had to have the courage of your disillusionments. No more the S&M clinch, the waltz of death. Ruthlessness was an art. He regretted everything, but not this.

The sky was darkening, yet he felt a new propulsive energy, formless and uncompetitive. Run, run, run, said all the pop songs he'd grown up on. He would take that advice, while never forgetting that anyone who is running from something is running towards something else.

I Am the Future Boy

I say to my youngest son, please, let's run together this afternoon. Sitting down exhausts me; some movement would do me good, we will feel the better for it – just twice around the Green, no more than fifteen or twenty minutes. I want to add: I'm losing strength, and boredom is worse as you get older. Mixed with sadness and regret, it seems heavier and more final; sometimes even music doesn't temper it. I wonder if a jog might dislodge some of my gloom.

For him this is a cue for sighing. It will be an effort; he will have to rise from the sofa and even leave the house. This short run could also be – this is his fear – an opportunity for me to lecture him on philosophical or psychological matters, or worse, politeness, sex or tidying up the house. Often he regrets that I exist at all, and that he has to deal with me.

But, miraculously, and to my surprise, he agrees.

We have done this before, and sometimes, as I trot along, he walks or even strolls beside me, rather patronisingly, in my view. But today, to equalise things, to make them more of an exertion and challenge, since I am so slow for this quick fifteen-year-old, he decides to strap on his ankle weights. They are heavy, pull at the muscles of the legs and cramp the ankles. For me, to wear such things would be like trying to cook while being crucified, but he has heard that this is how Cristiano Ronaldo practises step-overs.

Now, today, as we jog easily along the perimeter of the Green, I decide to give the little shit a shock, by kicking off a bit, insofar as I can. So I go a bit faster, and feel him fall behind me. I still have it, I think. I will sprint home in triumph, showing him who is boss.

In India, according to family legend, my father had been an excellent cricketer, boxer and squash player. I'd always run with him in our local park in the suburbs, until one day in the late 60s my father and I raced across the park to the open-air swimming pool, which was, more or less, the only other entertainment in the area. When I finished, and turned to look for him, his hands were on his knees and he was puffing wildly. I'd beaten him, and suddenly he seemed frail and vulnerable. I guess he might have been ill already, and he was to be sick for most of my teenage years. I ascribed huge and mysterious knowledge to my father, and still do. I didn't want to be disappointed. But I was at an age when I had to look forward. It is, however, a shock to learn that not only are your parents not the only people in the world, but that they are not even the most important to you.

And it is a shock for them when they see that you have seen this.

*

My youngest son runs easily beside me as we go. Once small for his age, this summer he has begun to develop a wide chest and long legs. Neighbours are startled by how tall he has suddenly become. We can look one another directly in the eye. Despite still having some of his baby teeth, he will soon have the body which every adult will spend his life trying to regain. His hair, until recently cut with some inaccuracy by his mother, has become a matter of interest and concern. I have started to take him to my barber, Luka, who works nearby out of a shabby cabin under a disused garage where my older teenage sons have their hair cut. Now and again they are also shaved by Luka, a man we consider the Lionel Messi of the razor, though we all tend to look a little Luka-like now. My youngest had Luka shave a sharp parting into his head. The boy is keen to look good now, and he gives Luka instructions, returning if the parting doesn't hold and having it recut.

D. W. Winnicott writes in *Playing and Reality* about a 'string boy', who ties everything together because of his terror of separation from his mother. I recall that one of my older sons went everywhere with a lasso for a long time. My youngest was once obsessed by string, until the house resembled a cat's cradle, with everything kept both together and apart, joined and not joined – just so, or carefully mediated, in terms of distance. Even now Bob the Builder still swings in a rope noose from the banisters. Eventually the kid gave up the string, and, as we scamper along, I wonder if this important transition to individuality is managed by an umbilicus of invisible elastic. He is slowly increasing his distance from me. My fading, and his rising, make life possible.

*

For a bit I am left behind. I stop to tie my shoelaces and regain my breath. At my youngest son's age I was a scrawny mongrel kid struggling in a rough neighbourhood. Nervous, inhibited, insecure, moody, I could barely live with myself. But there was pop music, and books in the local library: the efficacy of words in joining things up – but only if they were written down. I could barely speak to anyone around me. I felt fortunate that near-silence was fashionable, and everyone was so stoned they could barely speak. I was beginning to write, and I had found a good teacher, an editor at a London publishing outfit who came to my house on Sundays to work with me on the novel I had begun writing. I got on with things, and was serious for my age; somehow I knew I had to be if I were to go out and find more life.

I recognise that writing is an altogether different sort

of thing from speaking. I wonder if it's a protection against having to speak. If writing creates an intimate relation with a future reader, it changes little around you. But speaking – the ability to ask for what you want, and directly to modify others – has to be a necessary form of power. There's no use in keeping your words to yourself. For me, however, parting with words was almost an impossibility. When I tried to open my mouth authentically I fell into a kind of anguished panic. Speaking would be a disaster, turning me into someone I no longer recognised, as if I didn't want inevitable change, or to become the new person that saying real words can make you into. And if I couldn't speak, I felt blocked and distant and angry. In silence you rot.

I needed, as the young do, to escape, and I went to work in the theatre. Silent and anguished or not, I would be a writer. Fuck everything else: it was art or nothing. Artists did whatever they wanted. I thought then, and probably still believe, that to be an artist was the finest thing anyone could be. I had pretty much failed at school. I blamed myself for the fact the teachers there couldn't entertain me. They hated the pupils, and the pointless system ran on threat, fear and punishment. We were being trained in obedience, and to be clerks. After, I worked in offices, and didn't fit in there either. What sort of future would I have? If I couldn't imagine having a conventional job, I would make things much more difficult for myself: my future, everything, would depend on one throw of the dice. Looking back in puzzlement, it seems like blindness, stupidity, arrogance and very good sense. It takes a sort of mad courage to want something truly absurd.

Not that there hadn't been examples. At home I'd study photographs in magazines: Jagger and Richards swaggering and smoking outside some court or other; McCartney and Lennon in Hamburg and just after; Dylan around the *Blonde on Blonde* period. Defiant, original young men convinced of their own potency, desirability and immortality. Not only do these boys look as if they have just joyfully killed the old and now have the world to themselves, but to be a young man in the 1960s was to glimpse the view from a briefly opened window, to grasp an opportunity between two dependencies and enjoy a burst of libidinous freedom, of self-wonder and self-display.

These kids look free. But of what? Of the fetish of renunciation; of the dull norms and values of the day – whatever they were. Hadn't there been two relatively recent world wars through which our parents and grandparents had suffered, and for which generations of young men had had their natural aggression taken advantage of, and for which they had been sacrificed? You cannot forget, too, the sheer amount of daily fear, if not trauma, the child – any child – has to endure. You could also say that the teenager's life so far has been a cyclone of outrageous demands: to eat, shit, shut up and go to school; to behave well, to be obedient and polite while achieving this, that or the other; to go to sleep, wake up, take an exam, learn an instrument, listen to one parent, ignore the other, get along with one's siblings and aunts, and so on. And these compulsions and demands: one succeeds in obeying them, succeeds in failing them, or evades them altogether. But each of them will generate anxiety since they are all combined with punishment, fear and guilt. Stress will be the common condition of adulthood if the demand has been the constant of childhood.

Of course, the demand is the currency of all intercourse, and not all demands are impossible, pointless or demeaning. One wouldn't be a person unless one received or made them. These demands never end, either. At least in the West since the 1960s there might be fewer moral prohibitions than before. But there are more impossible demands. What isn't forbidden is almost obligatory: the prescription that one should be wealthy, or always active, or successful, or have frequent high-quality sex for all of one's life with someone beautiful is as likely to cause anxiety as any prohibition.

*

Anyone will notice that adults can lose their modesty when describing the achievements of their kids. Since the child is them but also not-them, the parent is free to brag. What sort of strange love is this, the parent's for the child, or what sort of possession is the child for the parent? Who or what does the parent want the child to be? What sort of ideal image do they have, and how can the child escape being devoured by the parent, or respond to them creatively?

Both my parents had fantasies of being artists of some kind, in writing, theatre, dance. But they were vulnerable emotionally and financially, had few opportunities, and seemed to stew in frustration, particularly as they got older. It was all talk, the dream of a life. They couldn't take any risks, and since they could afford to give nothing up, nothing was ever accomplished. Confined and restless, I saw I had to take their dreams for reality – and quickly, before I was done for. I liked to read and work; I wasn't afraid to be alone and I wanted to go far into England, to see what kind of country my father had come to and what we new arrivals would make it into. It was as an artist that I felt most individual, competitive, alive and envious of others' successes. If we are forged and made in difficulty, writing was a problem I wanted to take on. I barely thought about money or survival or security. We were hippies, and 'bread', at first, was never the aim of my very politicised generation, even after the deprivation of the post-war period. However, during the latter part of my lifetime it seems to have been decided that economic productivity and materialism are the ethics of choice, as the virtuous end of life. Now the teenager might be free sexually, but the neo-liberal project of open-ended economic success makes for scarcity, and for a severe form of insecurity and servitude.

*

I had my mirror years, and even fancied myself. For a time I was in love with what I saw. These were the days when everyone had more or less the same body shape. We all ate the same food, did the same amount of exercise at school, and how you looked was either good or bad luck, though as any Teddy boy could tell you, there was sticky stuff you could put in your hair to make you stand out.

Teenagers don't need to be reminded that wherever they are, their body is with them as an object. Teenagers have always been keen on harming, piercing and marking themselves. Now they go to the gym and shave their bodies and wax their hair; they hyperventilate over blackheads and what they're eating, and look critically and in wonder at themselves and each other. My boys check other boys' bodies before they check the girls. In this exile, this period of freedom between loves, hypereroticised, wild hedonists, they can really only love themselves. One day they will look at photographs of their younger selves and be shocked by everything they couldn't see or appreciate in themselves. And however beautiful they might be, any adult will remember that most of us when young felt a lot like Holden Caulfield or Esther Greenwood in *The Bell Jar*, awkward, not ready for the world, and disputing with our too-present or too-absent parents, to draw them closer, or push them away.

The age of fifteen to twenty in a kid is tough for a parent, with many cruel exchanges. The art the young are fascinated by – pop, hip-hop, video games, vile jokes, horror films – looks gratuitously sadistic. If they are fortunate enough to be able to develop all their capacities, our children, among other things, will have to become aggressive and even destructive. It is shocking, the way they say 'fuck you' all the time and mean it. Their necessary hatred, from the parent's point of view, seems so final. But it is nothing like the cruelty of adults, and this sudden invasion of the nasty and unkind, of a particularly unpleasant version of reality, is an important break from the past, a form of entry into the grown-up world. The machines the kids prefer to real people – computers, phones, video games – are transitional objects for semi-adults, and function as links between life stages.

But there is something else at this time, equally violent or shocking in its own way, a shock which perhaps never diminishes, and which pornography inadequately reproduces but also illustrates. I mean the radical disturbance of sex in its aggression and need. Of how violent, gross and hateful sex can seem, or needs to be, if one is to be abandoned in it.

44

For me this initiation was not only into my own sexuality, but a move away from adolescent solitude and narcissism – towards a woman, women, and more interesting dangers. This is one of the most difficult and important questions for a young man: how do you engage with or understand female sexuality? My parents' relationship never seemed sensual; it didn't appear to be that kind of love: they were companions who cared for one another. Appearance, yearning, or the game of love, didn't seem important to them, even in their speech.

Where do you learn how to desire, then? How do you allow a woman to teach you about their pleasure? At least I grasped that I would have to make a space for desire to occur. Then, I suppose, one just had to pay attention. Living more authentically, and being more politicised and aware of their situation and who they were – women becoming subjects in their own right, as it would have been put then – the women I knew were far ahead in the way they considered their identity and what they wanted to be.

I was afraid of excitement, of women, of sex, of losing my bearings and my mind. I must have been seventeen when a woman gave me acid, pulled up her top and invited me to lie down so she could masturbate me. She did it slowly, almost as an exercise, to show me what was possible, how she might control me and how I could learn to synthesise pleasure. Lying there, I witnessed her concentration, and then I let go and tripped in my head. At the end I felt paralysed, and it took me a few minutes to learn to walk again. A little older than me and more knowledgeable about everything, she was experienced enough to say – when I came round – that that wasn't all.

There was something else. It was, she explained, difficult for her to masturbate in front of a man; she felt exposed and embarrassed. But if she could get over that, I might see something essential or even useful for the future. After all, it took a man to know a woman, to understand her needs and passion, to look at her as she wanted to be seen. So she pulled down her clothes and showed herself. You have to admire the nerve of someone who could do that. She came quickly, and a few times more. I held and kissed her, amazed and fascinated by the beauty and intensity of this form of education, and I wondered what she needed me for, and what I could be for her, if anything. She said, well, you can't hold your own hand, and you can't desire or make love to yourself, can you?

*

My father and I would walk in the park on the weekends. Dad always had the immigrant's optimism. He believed we ought to succeed in the new country; that was why he wanted to be here. Yet I still don't know how his conversations were so inspiring. It was a great thing he had, knowing how to make you excited about the future, about what could be achieved and the pleasures which were possible. Not, of course, that you were allowed to leave him behind. My father, neglected by his own father, indeed by both his parents, broke and re-established the trans-generational inheritance, and became a good father himself. Yet he required his children as friends and accomplices. Now I am like him, and much different. He's long dead but every day I am in conversation with him. I'd like him to be here so I could kiss him or kill him.

*

My youngest son and I, on our run, slow down. My legs are tired; we walk together. I like to walk slowly. This is how we can talk about schools, sports, magic tricks, concentration, his friends, and how he'd never read anything I'd written. It's a lovely long moment between conflicts. From the parent's perspective, it is not hard to frighten or control young children, even when they are maddening. But – difficult to intimidate and almost impossible to charm – teenagers generate more hate, rage and envy than even the steadiest people can bear. A teenager can turn a fine person into a maniac in ten seconds. The more they need you the more anger they might need to get away – hatred is an important catalyst for change – and you can only have power over those who are dependent on you. You'll never get anywhere with a teenager by

47

appealing to your own interests, but they usually respond to money, and if you can involve them in something they like, or want to say, they can, for a bit, be good, amusing company.

There is a lot here for the parent to learn about separation. For what the kid sees as growing up and freedom is, from the angle of the parent, a fatal break-up. During the long divorce of the child's teenage years, it can feel as if you are slowly being deserted by one of your dearest friends. You will ask yourself what is left now you have almost completed this job. I can recall wondering at the time I left home, in the mid-70s, who my father would discuss literature and sport with.

Now I must remind myself, since Muslim fathers are very present, that I am the son of a mother too. Not that my mother much enjoyed being maternal; it was all a nuisance. She liked us as an excuse or obstacle, so we could appear to be in the way of something better. Yet when we were gone, nothing new happened. At the time I was leaving home, Mother seemed to become defensive and almost inert, as if she'd lost her vitality under layers of her own body. Television had been a novelty when I was a kid; we were amazed it existed at all. Soon Mum barely moved from the intoxicant of the TV, which she watched with increasing avidity. To me, she had fallen in love with something or, indeed, someone else, an insidious thing, a shadow-world, which appeared to provide no suffering or condemnation, unlike sex or alcohol, but only a constant, mild level of diversion. Eternally distracted by the only truly living figures in what we misguidedly called the living room, it soon seemed as if television was the single life which could compel her – people on a screen she couldn't actually reach and didn't have to talk to. In a way, I had lost both my parents.

The lesson here might be: you cannot use your kid or your parents as a prop, as a substitute for other relationships, or as a reason for not relating as an adult to other adults. Even parents have to grow up.

*

What will be significant in a life can't be discovered in advance, or even at the time. Meaning, trauma even, is a later construction arising from a realisation. I mean that people experience some sort of pain or feeling of loss; they know there's been some inexplicable breach, but they don't know exactly what it means. A writer, like a dreamer, is an 'interpreter' of experience, which makes writing an important form of thought, inscribing an event in the right place in the narrative you're using at the time, or opening a space for a new one.

Speaking is easier than writing. There are no 'creative speaking' classes, though there should be. The danger and virtue of speaking is incontinence or spontaneity – speaking as a form of unpredictable performance. Most people can speak, they rarely stop, they need to get it out. You can't really plan a conversation; it's an improvisation made by at least two, and truth escapes through one's fingertips. Someone can pull you through your defences, like picking a winkle.

Writing appears to be more manageable. Writing, like reading, is usually done in solitude, and there is nothing natural about it. Since people are their own obstacles and like to undermine themselves, it is an effort in overcoming. To write is to find out if you can be less afraid of yourself, less inhibited – freer, wilder, and yet able to structure your work. A thought occurs; you put it down, and revise it a dozen times, and then another ten. Most people can't write well; it's awkward, slow work, when done by hand. For me that is the best way, especially at the beginning of a project, when slowness and thought matter. Since it is abstract and self-conscious, as well as a form of separation and withdrawal, writing disconnects you from experience, freezing it. Sometimes this disconnection can feel like a sort of killing. Some young writers can even feel that if they write from their own life, or about their own family, that this objectification can be like murdering your own parents. They are rightly nervous of the amount of conflict and aggression which creative exploration seems to invite. No wonder they can feel inhibited. It's easier to avoid difference and the problem of taking power, to play dead and choose to be passive or submissive, than to argue or be individual. But the price is higher.

*

For young writers there is no audience. No one real hears them yet. They have to attempt difficult things. They must work at ideas which are beyond them. It would be sensible for them to find a good teacher, one who would push them. That would be their apprenticeship, when they would be rejected, criticised and knocked down repeatedly, as they would be in the world. Most of the young writers I teach don't produce enough work. They're over-anxious about the quality of what they're doing, not bold enough, and, later on in the process, not tough enough when it comes to cutting and rewriting.

But at least if you can see writing as a form of costume or masking, you can see that it can be learned. The voice, the point of view, is a put-on. All this is pretence, a form of magical play, like string-work with more omnipotence. Even forms of recently fashionable 'confessional' writing, which appear to be told like it was, require as much art and construction as any thriller, which is why often these pieces turn out to be more fictional than intended. And this is more than just expressing oneself. The writer is a fiction, having created herself out of what she has been given.

I would go further. When you write, you are addressing other people; there is always someone else there, someone who sees you. And this absent reader whom the writer imagines – the subject the writer is trying to take on an outing, the implicit receiver of the words, the one who should understand – is also a fiction, an essential one. This fiction orientates the writer. The reader makes the writer possible. Yet thinking of the reader makes the writer anxious. This reader is judging you. This reader recognises you, and reads you properly. The reader wants to be fascinated and enchanted. This is the crucial question for the writer, as it is for any person. How do we keep the other's attention? How do we keep their desire for us alive? What do they see, and do they love us? Will they forgive us our mistakes? Are we giving them something they want, something they don't want, or something else altogether? Living with such anxiety, and answering it back, justifying your work, is necessary to the process.

Some writers think their characters have to be sympathetic. That is not at all necessary or common in good writing, and cute characters are off-putting. Obviously, you'd no more read a book on the basis of its characters being likeable than you'd choose a lover because they were nice. All that must happen is for the reader to become involved with the writer's people, and see themselves in the conflicts and dilemmas the writer produces.

*

The devilish character Jack Tanner in George Bernard Shaw's *Man and Superman* states, 'The true artist will let his wife starve, his children go barefoot, his mother drudge for his living at seventy, sooner than work at anything but his art.'

In his witty essay 'The Writer on Holiday', Roland Barthes considers this romantic idea of the place of the writer in the public imagination. If writers are 'specialists of the human soul' or 'professionals of inspiration', the writer simply cannot go on holiday like other workers because he – and it is usually a he – isn't someone with a job. Art is a calling. A real writer is always a writer, and he can't help it, he just has to do it. This kind of pure artist – Shelley, Rimbaud, Van Gogh, Kafka, Plath, Nina Simone or the young Dylan, say – can't leave himself behind, or turn off his mind, since you can't cancel your subscription to inspiration. The Muse is a sort of 'inner tyrant'. And not only is the artist possessed, he must pay a high price for his devotion. He should sacrifice not only his time and financial security, but should also forsake the safety of being a good person. Mad and difficult, he must place his work before his wife and children, whom he would rather see ruined than compromise his will.

This amusingly misleading but not uncommon notion of the artist a moment away from hacking off his own ear prevents us from seeing art where it mostly is: in the market, in collaborationist if not negotiated forms like pop and the cinema, and in most types of craft. The written word, and the story, is still fundamental to us. Everything we see on TV or in the cinema, and every song we hear, was written down first. The idea of the romantic artist separates the use of the imagination from the rest of the public. The idealisation of the artist is a limitation which leads to impoverishment elsewhere, and can cause us to forget that the imagination extends to all areas of life.

*

Recently it has become common in film and television, and also in the novel, for the story idea to be based on the lives of real people. These are usually celebrities of some sort, often enduring a particularly dramatic period in their lives. It could be Nelson Mandela, Princess Diana, Tony Blair, Queen Elizabeth the First, Virginia Woolf, Sylvia Plath, Van Gogh, or a sportsman, actor or murderer. Mad poets and mathematicians are popular, nicely illustrating the popular idea that genius and idiocy are never far apart. For a producer or a writer, this can seem like a good solution to the problem of finding a story. Most of the work has been done. The characters already exist in the public imagination; the action has taken place, and the writer will have a good idea of how these people might speak and what they might say.

Most of this sort of writing is market-driven and is often commercial. On the other hand, the writing schools are full of middle-aged women who have growing kids. These eager students have turned to creative writing not to become well-off by working in television, but rather to find out – using the medicine of art – how they became who they are. They know that sanity depends on language, and writing is, as much as anything, a form of working meditation. There is, in silence with one's thoughts, an opportunity for memory to work. At the same time, to study writing in a university makes art appear arduous and respectable. Essays are written and classes are attended, and you leave the university stamped with credits. It is as if writing is an academic discipline rather than a species of unpredictable entertainment and psychic stripping, by which an audience may or may not be impressed.

The university gives a necessary semblance of respectability. If men are martyrs for their art, women like to be martyred for their children. They cannot suffer enough; it is a mark of love. How torn they are between the page and the kid. It is as if the parent's essential duty is to give the child everything until there is nothing left, rather than showing her the necessity of creativity and how important it might be to write – as a form of disruption, of internal reorganisation and recreation. Not that writing is a particularly masculine activity. Men are not better writers than women, but women can be more divided here. It might take a man to be ruthless enough to find the space and time to learn to write. Children can be a framework and a spur. If it is indulgent for any art to move too far from the market, and for the market to move too far from art, fatherhood makes you serious. It wasn't until I had children that I saw I had to concentrate. I had to get on with it, making more work, supporting the children with my pen, or find, for the first time, a proper job.

*

Now and again, to nicely devalue me, as if I've got the wrong idea about who I am, my youngest son will suddenly start to abuse me wildly in the foulest language, saying the hardest things he can think of. Then he looks at me nervously and asks, 'Are you still alive?' But today he is in a mild mood, and merely says, 'Come on, old fellow, don't give up, you can do it – maybe . . .'

He will run with fitter people, I tell him. But he doesn't like to compete with his friends, for fear of losing and being humiliated. I can only say that if you don't compete, you have already lost, that your conflicts make you, and that, if you can, you must welcome them. Yet he will have a lifetime of competition ahead of him: for friends, lovers, sex, jobs. Substituting the lost paradise of a secure childhood for the intenser vagaries of sex and love, he will win and lose. He will be envied, hated even; he will enjoy the pleasures of brutality, and will suffer from sexual jealousy; there's no cure for that, or for any of it.

*

At the end of the street I can see all he has been holding back. He turns it on, rushing along the pavement to the gate, 'destroying me', as he puts it, and laughing when I finally turn up.

At last we are home; he takes off the weights, and we both lie on our backs on the floor. We are together, and we are happy together for a while.

His Father's Excrement: Franz Kafka and the Power of the Insect

In the famous, reproachful 'Letter to His Father', which Franz Kafka wrote in 1919 but, characteristically, never delivered, the writer recalls an early memory in which the old man left the whimpering young boy on the balcony at night, 'outside the shut door', just because he wanted a drink of water.

'I mention it as typical of your methods of bringing up a child and their effect on me. I dare say I was quite obedient afterward at that period, but it did me inner harm . . . Even years afterward I suffered from the tormenting fancy that the huge man, my father, the ultimate authority, would come almost for no reason at all and take me out of bed in the night and carry me out onto the balcony, and that consequently I meant absolutely nothing as far as he was concerned.'

Far from being an absent, unimpressive father, Hermann Kafka was an overwhelming man: too noisy, too vital, too big, too present for his son, so much so that Franz was unable ever to abandon or break with him. Although Franz wrote in his diary, 'A man without a woman is no person,' and came close to marrying Felice

Bauer and, later, Julie Wohryzek, he could not become a husband or father himself. Franz Kafka was otherwise engaged: he and his father were locked in an eternal arm-wrestle.

Kafka takes the 'absolutely nothing' of his 'Letter' very seriously. In the two stories discussed here, 'The Metamorphosis' and 'A Hunger Artist', written seven years apart, this 'nothing' becomes literalised. Out of fury and frustration, Kafka's characters use their worthless bodies – these so-called 'nothings' – as a weapon, even as a suicide bomb, to destroy others and, in the end, themselves.

In 'The Metamorphosis', generally considered to be one of the greatest novellas ever written, and a foundation stone of early modernism, Gregor Samsa wakes up one morning to find he has become transformed from a human being – a hard-working travelling salesman, a son and a brother – into an insect, a bug, or a large dung beetle, depending on the translation. And in 'A Hunger Artist' the protagonist, a determined self-famisher, exhibits himself publicly in a cage, where, eventually, he starves himself to death as a form of public entertainment. Like Gregor Samsa in 'The Metamorphosis', at the conclusion of the story he is swept away, having also become 'nothing', a pile of rubbish or human excrement that everyone has become tired of. The hunger artist is replaced in his cage by a panther with 'a noble body', a fine animal the public flock to see.

As a young man, Franz Kafka, notoriously fastidious when it came to noise and food, became a follower of a Victorian eccentric called Horace Fletcher. (Henry James was also a 'fanatical' follower of Fletcher.) Known as 'The Great Masticator', Fletcher advocated 'Fletcherising', which involved the chewing of each portion of food at least a hundred times per minute, as an aid to digestion. (A shallot, apparently, took seven hundred chews.) Fletcher's disciple Franz Kafka was, on top of this, a vegetarian, in Prague, of all places. Hermann Kafka, on the other hand, was a man of appetite, who seems, from the outside, to have been hard-working, devoted to his family, loved by his wife, to whom he remained faithful, and a Czech-speaking Jew in a tough, anti-Semitic city. Certainly, Hermann had a more difficult childhood than his son, working from a young age, leaving home at fourteen, joining the army at nineteen, and eventually moving to Prague to open a fancy-goods shop. His two youngest sons died in childhood and his daughters would die in the concentration camps.

Hermann's surviving, sickly, scribbling, neurotic first son, Franz, something of an eternal teenager, appears to be what might now be called an anorexic. Despite the fact his mother blithely considered him healthy, and refused to fall for the 'performance' of his numerous illnesses, there wasn't much he could digest; it was always all too much. The boy was certainly strong in his own way; he was pig-headed and stubborn, a refusal artist of some sort, and he was not unusual in that. There are many kinds of starvation, deprivation and protest, and some of them had already become a form of circus.

A generation before, at the end of the nineteenth century, in the sprawling Salpêtrière hospital in Paris's thirteenth arrondissement, the psychiatrist Jean-Martin Charcot was overseeing another form of exhibitionism of the ill. It was mainly hysterical women he exhibited in his semi-circular amphitheatre on Tuesday afternoons, where 'all of Paris' – writers like Léon Daudet and Guy de Maupassant, along with interested doctors like Pierre Janet, Sigmund Freud and George Gilles de la Tourette, as well as socialites, journalists and the merely curious – came to stare at these strippers of the psyche. Some of the women were hypnotised by Charcot's interns; Charcot also publicly diagnosed patients he'd never met before. And while hysteria was mostly a disorder diagnosed by men and associated with women, there were a few male patients: one had been a wild man in a carnival; another worked in an iron cage at a fair, eating raw meat.

What sort of show was this, and what kind of staged illnesses did they suffer from, these weird somnambulists and contortionists, with their tics, paralysis, animalism and inexplicable outbreaks of shaking and crying? Were their conditions organic, or was it true that illness was merely misdirected sexuality? Were they ill at all, and, if so, which words best described them? And doesn't the physician, before he can heal, first have to wound?

After one of these crowd-pleasing occasions, and while researching 'Le Horla', his story of possession, Guy de Maupassant wrote in a newspaper article, 'We are all hysterics; we have been ever since Dr Charcot, that high priest of hysteria, that breeder of hysterics, began to maintain in his model establishment in the Salpêtrière a horde of nervous women whom he inoculates with madness and shortly turns into demoniacs.'

Sigmund Freud, studying in Paris for a few months, visited Charcot's home three times, where he was given cocaine to 'loosen his tongue', and was so impressed by him that he translated some of his works, and named one of his sons after him. But Freud was to take an important step on from Charcot. Rather than looking at women, he began to listen to them. From being avant-garde, living works of art, they became human beings with histories, traumas and desires. Rather than action, it was language, with its jokes, inflections, omissions, hesitations and silence which was the telling thing here. The mad are people who don't understand the rules, or play by the wrong rules, internal rather than official ones; they are heeding the wrong voices and following the wrong leaders. Yet the mad, of course, cannot do absolutely *any-thing*. Madness, like everything else, has to be learned, and, as with haircuts, when it comes to folly, there are different styles in fashion at the time. If madness, and questions about sanity and the nature of humanity, are *the* subject of twentieth-century literature – what is a person; what is health; what is rationality, normalcy, happiness? – there is also a link to theatre, and to exhibitionism. As a form of self-expression, it might be important to be mad, but it might also be significant that others witness this form of isolating distress, for it to exist in the common world, for it to be a show, moving and affecting others. More questions then begin to unravel. Who is sick in this particular collaboration, the watcher or the watched, the doctor or the patient? And what exactly is sick about any of them? Isn't the exclusive idealisation of normality and reason itself a form of madness? And if these exhibitionists wish to be seen, understood or recognised, what is it about themselves they want to be noticed?

Jean-Martin Charcot's 'living sculptures', as one might characterise them, these divas on the verge of madness – those who can only speak symptom-language – are not unlike Strindberg's female characters: fluid, disturbing, undecipherable, indefinable, oversexualised. (Kafka loved Strindberg, and writes in his diary, 'I don't read him to read him, but rather to lie on his breast. He sustains me.') Yet in their exhibitionism – the only communication they were encouraged in – these hysterics resemble the self-starver in 'A Hunger Artist'.

Most great writing is strange, extreme and uncanny, as bold, disturbing and other-worldly as nightmares: think of *One Thousand and One Nights*, *Hamlet*, 'The Nose', *The Brothers Karamazov*, *Oedipus*, *Alice in Wonderland*, *Frankenstein* or *The Picture of Dorian Gray*. If someone had never met any humans, but only read their novels, they'd get an odd idea of how things go here on earth: a series of overlapping madnesses, perhaps. Kafka is no exception when it comes to comic exaggeration, using the unlikely and bizarrely untrue to capture a truth about ordinary life.

However, in most magical tales of imaginative transformation, the subject of the story becomes bigger or greater than he is already, a superhero of some sort, with extra powers: a boy wishing to be a big man. One of the puzzles, ironies and originalities of 'The Metamorphosis' is that the alteration is a diminishment. Kafka is canny enough to take his metaphors literally, to crash together the ordinary and the unreal, the demotic and the fantastical. He doesn't, after all, tell us that Gregor feels like a dung beetle in his father's house, but rather that one morning Gregor wakes up to find he has actually become a dung beetle. As with Charcot's hysterics, Gregor had become alien to his family and the world, and the story tells us that almost any one of us could wake up in the morning and find ourselves to be foreign, not least to ourselves, and that our bodies are somewhere beyond us, as strange as our minds, and, like them, also barely within our agency.

'What shall I become through my animal?' Kafka asks in 1917, in *The Blue Octavo Notebooks*. He no longer wants to be either an adult or a man. And we might ask of the hunger artist, whose body is also destroyed, what sort of diminished thing does he want to be? Is he a starving saint, idiot, or sacrificial victim? Self-harm is the safest form of violence; you are, at least, no danger to anyone else. No one will seek revenge. To starve oneself, or to become a bug, is to evacuate one's character, to annihilate one's history and render oneself a void. But what are these transformations in aid of? Is this living sculpture showing us that we ask for too much, or showing us how little we need? What sort of demonstration is this spiritual anorexic engaged in?

The hunger artist's 'bodywork' resembles some of the 'performance' art of the twentieth century, which existed outside the conventional museum, and was probably most influential in the 1970s. Human bodies had been torn apart in the wars, revolutions, medical experiments, pogroms and holocausts of the twentieth century. Subsequently, artists who had formerly disappeared behind their ideas would become overt autobiographers, literally using their bodies as their canvas or material, mutilating, cutting, photographing or otherwise displaying themselves before an audience, a 'theatre of torture', if you like, showing us the ways in which our bodies are a record of our experience, as well as what we like to do to one another.

Kafka, who loved theatre and cabaret, and hated his own 'puny' body, particularly in comparison to his father's hardy, 'huge' physique, was more interested in the tortured male frame than the female form. Not that Kafka wasn't interested in women, and not that he didn't torture them. This was a pleasure even he could not deny himself. As is clear from his many letters, he practised and developed this fine art for a long time, until he became very good at maddening, provoking and denying women. He also went to enormous trouble to ensure that none of the women engaged with him was ever happy or satisfied. In case she got the wrong idea, or, worse, the right one – that he was a panther masquerading as a bug – Kafka pre-emptively describes himself, to his translator and friend Milena Jesenská in 1919, as an 'unclean pest'.

Kafka met Felice Bauer at Max Brod's in 1912. She must have panicked him, since soon afterwards he wrote 'The Metamorphosis' in three weeks, quickly making it clear that he would rather be a bug or a skeleton than an object of female desire. He made sure, too, never to write a great woman character. Kafka could not portray the eroticised, sexually awakened subject; the body was always impossible and a horror, and he worked hard all his life to remain a grotesque infirm child. Too much love and sexual excitement on both sides would have been exposed, and Kafka, the paradigmatic writer of the twentieth century, is, above all, a writer of resentment, if not hatred. In his world view – and all artists have a basic implicit fantasy which marks the limits and possibilities of what they might do – there are only bullies and victims; nothing more. The women had to learn, repeatedly, what it was like to be refused. No woman was going to get a drink of water from Franz Kafka.

Yet Kafka constantly solicited information from his women, making them 'captive by writing', as he put it in a letter to Brod. He insisted they follow his instructions; he always wanted to know 'everything', as he puts it, about a woman. There is, of course, nothing in this kind of ceaseless 'knowing'. There is no actual knowledge in such a heap of facts, and certainly no pleasure, exchange, laughter or unpredictability. Kafka preferred to eroticise indecision and circling; he came to love 'a long uncertain waiting', and he never possessed the women he loved. He wanted to be their tyrant, not their equal. After all, he knew tyrants: he had lived with them. And he, the kindest of men, tyrannised mainly himself until everything became impossible. He would chew and chew until his food was fit only for a baby, but he would rarely swallow. Likewise, the women would ride on Zeno's arrow forever, never arriving, never getting anywhere at all, always on the way – to nowhere.

Kafka's writing, his diaries, letters, notebooks, stories and novels, as well as his personal life, have become one work or dream. They were his self-analysis and his social and sexual intercourse. He made everyone up out of words: Felice, Milena, Gregor, Joseph K, and himself. The child even created his own parents. Kafka's father, the supposed super-tyrant, who told his son he would 'tear him apart like a fish', was one of Franz Kafka's liveliest lies, probably one of his best literary creations or fictions. Kafka might have turned himself into a bug, but he transformed his father into a text. Throughout literature, the two of them would be an immortal double-act, always co-dependents, like Lucky and Pozzo in *Waiting for Godot*, unable to live with or without one another, dancing together forever. So, when Hermann deprived his son of a drink, when Hermann became the master who could make the slave die, food and nourishment became the son's enemy, and deprivation and failure his subject. Kafka has more in common with Beckett than he does with Joyce or Proust when it comes to a world view. He and Beckett are both philosophers of the abject, of humiliation, degradation and death-in-life, just right for the twentieth century, a time of authoritarian fathers and totalitarian fascists, the weak and the strong, generating one another.

If you want to control others, either you can use strength or you can try weakness. Both methods have their drawbacks and particular blisses. Kafka's father took one position, and the son the other. It was a perfect division of labour, a torture machine which always worked. Franz rebelled against Hermann, complaining about him ceaselessly, as he appeared to rebel against families and marriage. But he only complained because he never found a father, family or marriage that he liked – just as the hunger artist claimed he never found any food which appealed to him. Otherwise, he claims, he would have eaten.

So Kafka grumbled, protested and rebelled, but he never revolted. He never overthrew the system or sought to do away with it, to escape the impasse and start afresh in another place with another family, making new mistakes. Perhaps none of us can forsake our love of the stand-off. Kafka refers to his father as 'the measure of all things for me' but also calls him weak, 'with a nervous heart condition', which, presumably, was why Franz wrote rather than spoke to him. Franz sensed his father's vulnerability; a sick father is doubly dangerous for an ambitious son. In order to hate him, Franz needed to keep him alive, and he needed to ensure his father would always have the advantage over him. The father had to remain powerful. Unlike Franz, Hermann was loved steadfastly by a loyal woman for his entire adult life. The son was sure to die first.

These stories by Kafka are important, and so resonant and unimpeachable when it comes to their place in world literature, because they expose a familiar self-destructiveness involved in trying to please or punish the other. As with any ascetic, or the figures Freud in his essay on Dostoevsky calls 'criminal', Kafka and his characters, these victims of themselves, came in time to learn to love but also to utilise the punishment they required. This hysterical martyrdom became an area of minimal enjoyment and freedom, where they and other marginalised subjects – women, Jews, writers – could dose themselves with the cool love of pain whenever they wished. They could, too, torture the other while remaining innocent, forever a victim. Kafka liked to remain a slave, while attempting indirectly, through writing, to control the master. Not long after reading Dostoevsky's *Notes from Underground* in 1887, Nietzsche writes of this sort of malevolent, resenting figure in *On the Genealogy of Morals*: 'Intoxicated by his own malice . . . his spirit loves hiding places, secret paths and back doors. Everything covert entices him as his world . . . Man suffers from himself, and is like an animal in a cage . . .'

The abject believe that their suffering is sacred and a virtue, that their sacrifice will save the other, and, ultimately, themselves. In 'The Metamorphosis' Gregor Samsa turns himself into an insect in order to ensure his family survives. Remember, there's nothing absurd about Kafka's characters. While they are, of course, obtaining huge satisfaction from being ill, and while their lascivious work of agony might seem futile, they are – at least in fantasy – busy saving lives, and at some personal cost. However, Gregor's father, understandably fed up with him, pelts him with apples, indicating perhaps that the boy could do, at least, with acquiring some balls. Eventually the son's corpse is swept out by the maid.

It was commonly believed that the world was dangerous, but that inside the desexualised family, where the kind, authoritative parents held everything together, all was safe. This was the bourgeois ideal of family happiness, a myth Freud helped destroy with his own story of love, desire and hate, the Oedipus Complex. Kafka illustrated Freud's tale in 'The Metamorphosis', the tale of what a youngster might have to do to survive within the complicated passion of a family, and what he might have to do to help ensure the others' survival. You can forget the police or racists: the people most dangerous to you are those you love, and who love you. Love can be worse than hate, a tender tyranny, when it comes to forms of control and sadism. After all, Kafka never says his father doesn't love him.

Towards the end of his life, while thinking about education, Kafka cited the myth of Kronos, who devoured his own children after they were born to prevent them overthrowing him, after he had previously cut off the genitals of his own father. Is education about flourishing, or is it about constraint, punishment and policing? What does the parent want the child to be?

However, 'The Metamorphosis' is not merely a tale of how mad, envious, indifferent or just ordinary parents can limit a child's imagination and sense of possibility. Kafka's texts, unlike his relationships, are endlessly fertile and open. No artist knows quite what they're saying: the world blows through them, and, if they're lucky, they might catch a scrap of it, which they will shape and remake, but without entirely grasping the entire truth of the thing. Saying and meaning are never the same. Hence, 'The Metamorphosis' can be read differently, the other way round entirely.

It is in this reversal that we see 'The Metamorphosis' as a terrible amusement, a black comedy, illustrating how one sick member of a family, seemingly the weakest one, can control, manipulate or mesmerise the rest, and there isn't much the others can do about it without appearing cruel or becoming consumed by guilt. As with the maestro Charcot's surreal displays at the Salpêtrière – a 'production line of madness' – 'The Metamorphosis' is also about the fascinating power of the ill and the spell they can cast. The story concerns the creativity of illness and the mutability of the self, and what a powerful tool sickness is, one which is rarely used just by the merely incapacitated. Nietzsche calls man 'the sick' animal, and for him the sick, particularly the 'purposefully' or unconsciously sick, are a hazard, absolutely lethal in their sadistic power. After all, in time the West would become pathologised in its emotional tenor, and almost everyone at one point or another would claim to be a victim of their history, a subject of trauma, and helpless in the grasp of the past. There would be a veritable proliferation or plague of diagnoses from numerous 'experts' – counsellors, psychologists, psychiatrists – many directed at children. Illness, equated with innocence, would be everywhere, until the world resembled a hospital.

At the conclusion of 'The Metamorphosis', when Gregor is dead and his corpse swept away by a servant, the family seem liberated and revived. They leave the apartment at last, and indeed the town. Kafka, not normally associated with happy, healthy endings, writes ecstatically, 'The tram, in which they were the only passengers, was filled with warm sunshine. Leaning comfortably back in their seats they canvassed their prospects for the future, and it appeared on closer inspection that these were not at all bad.'

In Kafka's 1914 story 'In the Penal Colony', a condemned prisoner's body is literally written on with a poisoned dagger-like pen, over twelve hours, until he dies, thus bringing together in one tale Kafka's favourite themes. As we know, outside of writing, Kafka's preferred site of activity was the body, about which he obsessed. But if Kafka preferred somatic solutions to political ones, we must not forget that something else was going on – something important. It was the beetle, the sick son himself, who was both recording this and inventing the story as a consolidated picture of what went on. Who, after all, could tell this family's story? Who had the right? And from which point of view? No one authorises a writer to be a writer. Certificates of excellence cannot be handed out here. He or she has to be their own authority and guarantor. With Kafka, the 'weakest' member of the family kept the ledger, and his imposed vision prevailed. He had the talent to demand complicity from the reader.

And there, in his writing, Kafka hid himself, while displaying himself for literary eternity. He spoke from where he hid. No one was going to get much love or even a glass of water, but they might get an amusing if not grim story, at least the ones which survived the destruction he appears to have half-heartedly requested. And Kafka kept on writing, until the end. This persistence showed the necessity of writing, and that some stories could seem like a cockroach in the room, reminding us of that which we prefer not to consider part of us. The intrinsic anarchy of real writing could become an attack, too, on total systems of thought, like Marxism or Nazism, or religion: always outside, the hysterics, masochists, bugs and self-starvers, despite their wish to be nothing, just would not fit into any comfortable place, always making people work to think about what they might signify.

It is a contemporary nostrum that writing might organise and advance people's ideas, making for some clarity. Writing can function as a kind of therapy by exposing the unconscious. Write as it comes and you might get a glimpse of how you feel and who you really are. Writing, too, might also be some sort of appeal to the other, a letter pretending to be a novel. It might represent the hope of change, of engagement, of a future. If we are made of words, we can be undone by them; but we can also undo them.

'I am incapable of speaking,' Kafka announced in his diary and, of course, the insect in 'The Metamorphosis' is incomprehensible to his family, communicating only in a private language. Kafka told us often that he could not speak, for fear, presumably, that something might happen. Speaking and acting were the father's realm, and he left them to the old man. There were only certain circumstances in which Kafka could produce words, and writing was something his father did not do. So writing was the single creativity and freedom Kafka allowed himself, though he was careful to ensure this creativity did not seep into his life or relationships. The question here has to be: what does writing do for the writer? What place does it have in his or her life?

Despite the purported therapeutic benefits of some forms of writing, Kafka's writing was not an attempted cure. None of his characters can change or be redeemed; they're tragic – their instincts will drive them inevitably to the zero point of death. Fate is a father, and he is inescapable. For Kafka, art became an important 'instead of', a substitute for speech and action. Transporting his inner world outside the magic circle of the family – and onto the page – writing both saved his life, and stopped him living. 'The Metamorphosis' and 'A Hunger Artist' show what you might become if you can't be an artist. These are, if you like, alternative lives. Not that Kafka merely hid out scribbling in his burrow of words. While writing, he wasn't afraid: at his desk he had few scruples about what he said, and his position was extreme and destructive. Kafka's characters are not timorous, weak or indecisive. They are powerful beings, and the alterations they choose have a dramatic effect. Kafka's work was a violent fantasised attack on himself and on the other, via his own body. He aestheticised his suffering, though even that wasn't satisfying enough. In the end, he had to attack the body of his own writing, apparently asking Brod to burn his unpublished work.

Writing could never be curative for Kafka; he was always as ill as he needed to be. Instead, writing was a fantasy of mastery, a kind of balancing act, keeping everything the same until he faded and died. Otherwise, life beyond Kafka's desk would always and only ever remain an altruistic masochism. Sometimes such narrowings are necessary. Kafka believed that it was in his words that he was at his best; writing was what he lived to do; he was 'made of literature' and he was omnipotent there, exerting control within the illusion of literature.

Kafka wrote in his diary in 1921: 'It's astounding how I have systematically destroyed myself . . .' Yet he and his readers were always aware of this Christ-like facade. His self-portrait as an insect, and the perverse insistence on innocence, ensured that his destructiveness was never a secret. Kafka repeatedly insisted on this self-cancelling and the shame it caused him. But he is never entirely convincing. He misled himself, as people do, for good reasons. There was more to his pose than he could know or own up to. He was always 'devilish', as he put it in the diary, 'in his innocence'. Don't the bug and the starving hunger artist attract much amazement and confused attention before they begin to bore their spectators? Don't they at least have an audience? And, look here, the characters seem to be saying, look at what you made me do to myself!

Not that the bug or the starving artist are all that Kafka is. While Kafka reminds us of important things – of the abuse of authority and the impossible stupidity of bureaucracy and of justice, of the ever-suffering body and the proximity of death, of how vile other people can seem – writers are bigger, more intelligent and almost always more creative than their characters. They have to be: the writer is the whole book and all the protagonists, not just a part of it. From his or her place at the centre of the scene, the writer sees behind the story, and ahead of it. In writing, the horror happens to one's characters, rather than to oneself. The writer cannot be the victim of this particular story, the story he is telling, because although a book might be a collection of possible fates, these are not the fates he will encounter. That is not the door he must go through.

Kafka wrote to Brod not long before he died, 'What I have play-acted is really going to happen.' His symptoms had finally become his life. Yet, despite his desperate protestations of hopelessness, his willed passivity and his penchant for victimisation, Kafka remained an omnipotent progenitor. The world is made of words, and he was the father of his texts, becoming his father's father, the one with the power, telling the story as he saw it and inviting the reader to take his side. A shaper and authority when it came to his fictional reality, he constructed, structured and organised an effective world, running every part of it. As with the ringmaster and showman Charcot's Tuesday performances, the entire scene was of the writer's making, and, like Charcot, he expected the audience's complicity, and for his interpretation to confirm his view of the world. Kafka was the master we still read: he was the weakest and the strongest, and, through his words, kept all of them – his family and his characters – alive forever.

The Wound and the Wand

I have come to adore my pens and can often be found fondling them, particularly my old classic Mont Blanc. But I have fallen for a new black Montegrappa, with its shiny case, heaviness and bendy nib. A favourite occupation of mine is to study the Montegrappa catalogue, turning the glossy pages slowly, convincing myself I need the turquoise one, and cannot survive another minute without the limited edition St Moritz. Not that expensive pens are always better than cheap ones. I use Lamy fountain pens every day, as well as their roller balls, in a variety of colours. Muji is excellent for light gel pens. But sometimes only a soft pencil will do . . . And still, a lot depends on the kind of paper you use and which nib runs best on what surface . . .

A writer could come to love the eventful paraphernalia of writing equipment and inks, of which colour where, as guitarists love guitars, photographers their cameras, and fetishists their thing. I like to see the page I'm on decorated. I want my art or craft – writing – to resemble a physical activity like drawing. This is not only passing time until one has to actually commit to the agony of beginning. In terms of sentences and paragraphs, I like the page to be prettily laid out; it is part of the pleasure of what I do, just as I like to look at art while I'm writing, rather than reading other people's words.

This pleasure, of course, is only a minor hedonism, for how could I forget that I grew up in the 1960s, when pleasure was still hidden, subversive and irreligious, when sucking on a cigarette could seem decadent? Recently, in my spare time, I've taken to lying on my sofa thinking of hedonists I admire – or admired. I think, in particular, of a good friend who died recently, a former roadie, private detective and storyteller – a man who could make the world seem worth getting up for – who explained last year to my youngest son and me, as we sat in Rio's Sugarloaf cafe, that he once fucked six women in a day. How hip it was in the 1960s, and particularly in the seventies, not to take care of yourself or anyone else, stepping as close as you could to peril and death, where things got raw and seemed to matter more than anything else: how important it was to be a threat to oneself, if not to others. The Velvet Underground, with their black polo-necks and near-death look, were an impressive influence. With dyed blond hair, Charlie Hero, in the television version of *The Buddha of Suburbia*, stalks the school playground with authority because he has the Velvet Underground and Nico album under his arm . . .

But as for committed hedonism, there's always the danger of there being too much of it. If, in certain circumstances, drugs can be bad for you, work can be worse. The ever-reliable Nietzsche, when it comes to truth, denotes work 'the best policeman' and pits work – mind-numbing labour – against more important matters like 'brooding, dreaming, worrying, loving, hating', suggesting that pure labour organises us too easily and excludes too much. We use work as a discipline to kill off our most interesting and passionate impulses.

If the most significant post-war literary text, *Waiting for Godot*, was about the unbearable heaviness of deferment, about how mad you can go when nothing important is happening, we grew up – in the mode of capitalism then fashionable – in a period of instant gratification. Waiting, and frustration, were no longer allowed. We wanted it all now, and we wanted it at once.

So beware: if there's only pleasure, it will call up destructiveness and death. Sacrifice is always a temptation. The pleasure-seekers explode, go crazy, or otherwise ruin themselves, as if that were the most perverse privilege of all. The natural end to pleasure would be addiction, a fatal narrowing, where one would find, at last, a boundary or a limit.

The important question has to be: how can we defend ourselves against our own destructiveness, those tantrums of the self-damned? How can we even see that we are being destructive? Where might we find better pictures of good lives?

The making of art represents the crossroads where the good things collide, where duty, magic and creativity fruitfully run into one another. Being an artist is a way of being interested in other people without having to sleep with them. There's an apt sentence by the British analyst Ella Sharpe: 'Sublimation is in its very externalisation an acknowledgement of powers within us to both love and hate.'

Not everything can be sublimated; one thing cannot be turned into another indefinitely. Nor can the excluded element be forgotten or renounced; it must find danger and an object or you will fall ill of unfulfilment, becoming unbearable to yourself. The hedonist, joy-rider and addict are safe from this; nothing new will happen since they have cancelled the future. They have ensured that the bad thing has already happened.

Making a swift survey, I see that friends who have endured with most contentment, if not happiness, are the artists or craftsmen, the ones who continue to work however futile it might feel. They go on: the work might be eccentric, far-out or delinquent, but the artist has to form and control her somersaults of the imagination to make something for others, enduring the frustration of turning day-dreaming into meaning. All work is productive, a greeting, a wave across an abyss, as the audience

84

overhears what the artist is going through.

The artist must live on the edge of failure. There can be no omniscience; any work could be a triumph, disaster or a bit of both. The difficulty here must be proportionate, and the work not impossible. The pen is a more than useful instrument; it is a wand which conjures that which you don't yet know into being.

The Art of Distraction

The other day it occurred to me that I needed more exercise and should take up skipping. I obtained a smart leather rope with weights in the handles, and, waiting until it was almost dark, went out into the street. Making sure that no one was coming, I started bouncing on the pavement. I must have skipped a bit as a child, I guess, because I could remember how to do it. Being a determined if not bloody-minded fellow, I improved after a few days; I could go on longer. But that was that: I didn't do more skips; my knees couldn't take it, and I soon ran out of breath. Nor could I do the leaps, twirls, step-overs and girly hops I'd seen on the internet. I repeated the same little leaden jumps over and over. Soon I had to conclude that I'd reached my level. The only way was down.

My thirteen-year-old son wandered out into the street and said he'd like to have a go with the rope, if I didn't mind. I handed it over and he began to fling himself in all directions at once, criss-crossing his arms, hopping and tripping from foot to foot while doing a Cossack impression; then he did the whole thing backwards, singing a Beatles song. It was moving and educational to be so instructed by one's son. I hoped an opportunity for retribution would soon present itself.

His easy display in comparison to my inefficiency stimulated in me childhood memories of being humiliated by my father at home in the London suburbs. In India Dad had, apparently, been brilliant at cricket, squash and boxing. As a young man I could never reach his level; nor did we have the facilities or sunshine to help provide the opportunity. Or perhaps Dad made sure I could not keep up with him. Whichever it was, my father, tragically, mostly wanted to be a writer and, it turned out, he wasn't great at that. He didn't give up, but he was never as good as he wanted to be, and his writing efforts yielded him little satisfaction or self-esteem, particularly as I began to succeed.

My son who can skip and sing found it difficult, for a long time, to read and write at the level of others his age. At primary school he was castigated, even insulted and punished for his inability. After experts were called in, he was investigated and berated some more, and finally labelled dyslexic and dyspraxic.

There is, at least, some relief in diagnosis. One is not alone, but joins a community of others who appear to have a similar condition. But can the inability to do a particular thing be described as a 'condition' at all? Would the fact I can't do the tango, read music or speak Russian be considered a 'condition'? Is it a failure of my development? Am I ill?

I wasn't much impressed by the imagination and curiosity of the experts: they used an awkward, objectifying language that sounded borrowed rather than earned, and none made the elementary connection between my competence at reading and writing, and the boy's inability, or refusal. And it usually isn't long, with an expert, before they begin to talk, fashionably, about brains and chemicals. Biological determinism is one of psychology's ugliest evasions, removing the poetic human from any issue.

An appeal to the certainties of science might seem finally to settle any question. But this is an ethical issue rather than a scientific one. It is values, not facts, which are at stake here. It is in the irritating human realm where the interesting difficulties are, and where one might have to really think about, and deal with, an individual's history, circumstances and reactions. It is the attempted standardisation of a human being and a limited notion of achievement which is limiting, prescriptive and bullying.

An eighteen-year-old acquaintance of one of my older boys mentioned that he'd been given Ritalin by a doctor, under his parents' instruction. He couldn't concentrate at school; his mind, he said, kept scattering off in numerous directions. He couldn't get anything done, and he was anxious that he was falling behind in life, and this was depressing him. I said that perhaps the teachers were dull, or that he had other, more pressing things on his mind. But he insisted that the drug focused him. He asked me whether, given the choice, I wouldn't prefer to focus at will.

This is a good question and I thought about the virtues of being focused, and what could be achieved with the full beam of concentration, within an intense charmed circle of attention, when the mind, feeling and will are linked. As a teenager, in particular, I wanted to be good at things, to shine, but, like the Ritalin boy, I fell badly behind at school, finding myself not only unable to learn but at the bottom of my class. I walked out of secondary school, and a semi-skinhead violent street culture, with three O levels, feeling as if I'd been badly beaten for five years. Fortunately I could tell myself it was still the late 60s, I was a rebel and didn't fit in – no one with any imagination could.

When I consider that wretched period now, I can see I wasn't enjoying a creative distraction, a vacation from the drudgery of a bad education, but was enduring a tantrum. Having shut myself off, I was suffering from a form of intellectual anorexia – the refusal to be given anything, to take anything in. As a result of that self-stymieing I lost hope and believed I'd never catch up or achieve anything. It was a short period in my life, but I haven't forgotten that early deficit. Sometimes I wonder if I'm still compensating for it. It was a relief for me eventually to discover some competence as a writer, though this was later, and it took me a long time to see its value, to understand that I had a gift and some intelligence, and that I might develop these, or even build my life around them.

When I was failing – and it was very isolating – I envied the love and accolades which the competent and the clever received. I thought that anyone would want such attention and admiration, and that it would lift their spirits. Competence, for me, was even preferable to beauty since any consideration received was earned and deserved.

For me, now, things do get done; books are finished, and other projects are started which are also finished. They take the time they take, and the breaks are as important as the continuities. Only a fool or an educationalist would think that someone should be able to bear boredom and frustration for long hours at a time and that this would be an achievement. Of course, without the ability to bear unpleasant affect, nothing is completed, but concentration follows interest and excitement, and the adults have a duty to give the kids good things, while the kids have to find a way to accept them.

What I might have said to my son's friend is that it is incontrovertible that sometimes things get done better when you're doing something else. If you're writing and you get stuck, and you then make tea, while waiting for the kettle to boil the chances are good ideas will spontaneously occur to you. Seeing that a sentence has to have a particular shape can't be forced; you have to wait for your own judgement to inform you, and it usually does, in time. Some interruptions are worth having if they create a space for something to work in the fertile unconscious. Indeed, some distractions are more than useful; they might be more like realisations, and can be as informative and multi-layered as dreams. They might be where the excitement is.

You could say that attention might have to be paid to intuition; that one can learn to attend to the hidden self, and there might be something there worth listening to. If the Ritalin boy prefers obedience to creativity – and who can blame him for wanting to cheer up the authorities? – he might be sacrificing his best interests in a way that might infuriate him later. A flighty mind could be going somewhere.

I might have been depressed as a teenager, but I wasn't beyond enjoying some beautiful distractions. Since my father had parked a large part of his library in my bedroom, when I was bored with studying I would pick up this or that volume and flip through it until I came upon something which interested me. I ended up finding, more or less randomly, fascinating things while supposedly doing something else. Similar things happened while listening to the radio, when I became aware of artists and musicians I'd never otherwise have heard of. I had at least learned that if I couldn't accept education from anyone else, I might just have to feed myself.

From this point of view – that of drift and dream; of looking out for interest, of following this or that because it seems alive – Ritalin and other forms of enforcement and psychological policing are the contemporary equivalent of the old practice of tying up children's hands in bed so they wouldn't touch their genitals. The parent stupefies the child for the parent's good. There is more to this than keeping out the interesting: there is the fantasy and terror that someone here will become pleasure's victim, disappearing into a spiral of enjoyment from which they will not return.

It is true, however, that many people, often called obsessives, have spent their lives being distracted, keeping away, often unknowingly, from that which they most want, thus brewing in themselves a poison of disappointment, bitterness and despair. But there are still, as the Ritalin boy seemed to know, forms of distraction which can be far more harmful. We can attack ourselves unknowingly: we might call this corrupted desire, as if we are possessed by a demon whose whispers are cruel diminutions of the self, destroying creativity and valuable connections, until enervation and self-hatred make a living death.

It is said that distractions are too easy to come by now that most writers use computers, though it's just as convenient to flee through the mind's window into fantasy. In the end, a person requires a method. I mean that he or she must be able to distinguish between creative and destructive distractions by the sort of taste they leave, whether they feel depleting or fulfilling. And this can only work if he is, as much as possible, in good communication with himself – if he is, as it were, on his own side, caring for himself imaginatively, an artist of his own life.

As we become desperate financially, and more regulated and conformist, our ideals of competence become more misleading and cruel, making people feel like losers. There might be more to our distractions than we realised we knew. We might need to be irresponsible. But to follow a distraction requires independence and disobedience; there will be anxiety in not completing something, in looking away, or in not looking where others prefer you to. This may be why most art is either collaborative – the cinema, pop, theatre, opera – or is made by individual artists supporting one another in various forms of loose arrangement, where people might find the solidarity and backing they need.

Weekends and Forevers

Marriage as a problem, and as a solution, has always been the central subject for drama, the novel and the cinema. Most of us come from a marriage, and, probably, a divorce, of some sort, and both bring together the most serious things: sex, love, children, betrayal, boredom, frustration, and property. The kind of questions which surround lengthy relationships – What is it like to live with another person for a long time? What do we expect? What do we need? What do we want? What is the relation between safety and excitement, for each of us? – are the most important we can ask.

Set in contemporary Paris, *Le Week-End* is a film I developed with the director Roger Michell, with whom I've worked on a TV series, *The Buddha of Suburbia*, and two films, *The Mother* and *Venus*. The films were mostly concerned with a subject we believed was neglected in the cinema: the lives and passions of older people, whose anxieties and desires, we found, were as intense, if not more significant, than those of the young.

Le Week-End concerns a late-middle-aged couple, Nick and Meg, who are both teachers, one in a school, the other in a university, and who go away to Paris to celebrate their thirtieth wedding anniversary. While there they discuss the meaning and direction of their marriage now their children have left home. Time and health are running out for them, as they consider their impending old age, and wonder what sort of future they might want, either together or apart. They think about how they might die, but this couple also need to talk about how they have lived: the way in which they have brought up their children, and how the family has worked, where it failed, and where there is regret, bitterness and even fury.

The film shows the depredations of time, but also the lability of the past, its different meaning and value for each of the couple, and how, now they are talking, it can seem as unstable as the future. They are looking in the same direction, but cannot see the same thing. There is no narrative they can agree on.

Their short sojourn, whatever else it is, will be a time of difficult conversations. What if it occurs to one or other of them that their relationship was a mistake, that it didn't resemble their original hopes at all, and they could have had a far better life elsewhere? Meanwhile, what have they done to one another? Was there harm? What did they use one another for?

The couple are from a suburb of Birmingham, where they have taught for decades. But 'Paris was where the twentieth century was,' says Gertrude Stein in *Paris*

France. And Paris, in their provincial English imaginations, represents several desirable things: the fresh ideas
and radicalism of the sixties and the barricades of 1968,
along with the intellectual revolutions of their youth
as exemplified by Derrida, Althusser, Lacan, Foucault.
There are also personal revolutions: the idea of the equal,
committed, but 'open relationship', represented by Jean-
Paul Sartre and Simone de Beauvoir, for whom 'the game
of love' – the rondo of seduction, rejection and change –
never had to end. As Stendhal writes in *Love*, 'The pleasures of private life ought to be augmented to an infinite
degree by recurrent exposure to danger.' But was it true
that love could easily be turned into a form of sport or
frivolous distraction? Surely love was no closer to sport
than sex was to exercise?

As well as these essential questions, Paris, for our
couple, represents continuity, and an ideal of civilisation. It means a certain quality of living when it comes
to clothes, sex, transgression, tolerance, conversation,
bohemianism. This pair like to eat well; it is in French
restaurants that they find sensuous enjoyment together,
perhaps the one place now where there is real collaboration and exchange between them.

In the London suburbs of the 50s and 60s, where I grew
up in relative safety after the turbulence of the war, all,
apparently, was set forever. Conventional marriage was
the paradigm. My father, an exile from colonial India's

religious strife and partition, was a commuter, and my mother was happy to call herself a housewife. The relation between work, marriage and play was perfectly arranged. Nothing was missing; it was all there already. All you had to do was fit in. That, at least, was the idea.

As Nick and Meg are aware, marriage frees a certain sort of companionate love, if you're lucky. But it domesticates sex. The couple are over-intimate. They know too much about one another. Without obstacles, there can be no fascination. How can you desire what you already have? That's not all: the arrangements which marriage requires to survive – security, duration, reliability, repetition – can seem liberating in their continuity, or stifling, according to your nature. The suburbs suited my father, since he'd come from a more dangerous place, and wanted contentment. But there was something about living there that could make you want to scream. For some, it would never be sufficient. You might learn, as Nick does in Paris with his wife – whom he still wants and needs – that the problem with desire is not that you cannot get rid of it, but that there is too much of it. It is ever-present, and ever-pressing, however much you want to discount it. You cannot wish it away, and it cannot be replaced by a substitute.

Either cannily or madly, John Cheever took up residence at the heart of the American Dream in a New York suburb, more affluent than the one I came from. He was a homosexual alcoholic artist attempting to be a straight married man. The mask and myth required to enact the gestures of servitude and constraint needed to live this kind of life proved disabling and humiliating. Cheever gave it a long try, and it enabled him to become an artist. But it never worked out; it was never going to. Chaos returned, and any fool could have predicted it would, even Cheever himself in certain moods. Perhaps there is only so much about yourself you can bear to understand.

A lot of this turns up in American writing at the time. And the question is always the same: was the repression worth it? Had too much that was essential been sacrificed for the ideal? How much of yourself could you give up and remain an 'authentic' person? Couldn't there be less painful or difficult, more satisfying ways to live, more in line with 'human nature', as the romantics might have put it?

An interesting version of someone wondering about this was Wilhelm Reich, the subject of a biography by Christopher Turner. A psychoanalyst trained by Freud in Vienna, and living in the US in the 50s, he and other 'liberationists' of the times, such as Norman O. Brown, Herbert Marcuse and R. D. Laing, were thinking about how desire could free people from oppressive and frustrating ways of living. According to Reich, the wrong life could make your body rigid, inflexible and awkward.

He says, in *The Function of the Orgasm*, 'that the average human being of today has lost contact with his real nature', and he writes of 'the incrustations and rigidities in human emotional life'.

Reich considered Freud conventional and pessimistic, and thought he didn't go far enough when it came to acknowledging the central place of sexuality in human life. For Freud, renunciation made some happiness possible, whereas Reich wanted to know why there had to be renunciation at all. Weren't human beings attacking that which in themselves was most alive: their capacity for love? Weren't fascist, authoritarian structures also inside the individual? Of course they were, argued Freud. But people loved their illness; they wanted to be unhappy; pleasure was the last thing they desired. A 'complete Eros', or ultimate cure, was impossible.

It wasn't long before Reich gave up on the most dangerous thing – speech – and the idea of the 'talking cure'. Speaking took too long; it was indirect and inconclusive. He began to touch his patients, believing that more and stronger orgasms were the solution. A full blast of pleasure, of orgiastic potency, would enable you to see you'd been living badly, or not according to your nature. This Salvationist view, from our less credulous and more cynical time, might seem like the least of it. But Reich was onto something here. If pleasure isn't your guide, what will be? Reich had some grasp of the creativity of sexual desire, and the cost of constraining it. And numerous people have been awoken from relative slumber by the unexpectedness of love or sex, and by the sense of opening out to more life and possibility.

I can recall a student of mine, a woman in her mid-forties, telling me a long, moving story about being 'awakened' emotionally, sexually and intellectually when she fell in love with a friend of her husband. Their love caused a huge trauma for both families, but it was worth it, she said. There would have been more suffering all round – wasted energy, unused love, unemployed passion – had she remained in the status quo.

The revolutionaries of the 60s called for new ways of being and alternative forms of social interaction. However, what the adulterer usually wants is better relationships, conversation, support, attention, pleasure. Her question is: how can we get what we want while behaving well, which means, at least, not being ashamed of ourselves?

The unhappy are no good to anyone. The unhappy are dangerous. The discontented and jaded become perverse or sadistic. Adulterers are not necessarily utopians: adultery merely shows the possibility of meaning, hope and love. My student didn't wish for anything like 'total liberation' – a revolution, a new social set-up – just for a satisfying marriage. And it is worth noting about the classic heroines of literature – Anna Karenina or Madame Bovary, or even the characters in David Lean's *Brief Encounter* – that they are not compulsive transgressors. They are asking for very little, and for everything, which, for them, is a fuller, more satisfying love. Complete happiness is a fiction, but some happiness is possible; indeed, it is essential. There are some people you can 'realise' yourself in relation to, and they are worth searching out. But there is a price. Something radical does have to change to make this possible – certainly, for women, in terms of the whole society – and there will be inescapable guilt.

Compared to Freud, Reich and his coevals prove, in the end, to be the more limited, if not conservative, concentrating on too small a notion of human need and fulfilment. Freud had a novelist's capaciousness; Reich was a headline writer. If constraint of some sort is impossible to avoid, the question is: which constraint, when, where?

Nick and Meg go to Paris because love is the most considerable business of all, and they need to know what sort of relationships make life worth living, and, if they have a future together, what it might be like. Do they suffer less together than they would apart? The decision they make at the end of the film can only be provisional, and the questions they ask have to be confronted repeatedly, since there isn't one answer that can satisfy them.

This Door Is Shut

More or less the last thing Farhana remembered before finding herself on the Boulevard Saint-Germain was her son Yasin waking up his driver and her guard, and ordering them to take her to Karachi airport. As Yasin was too drunk to drive her himself, he instructed the men to put Farhana on the 2 a.m. flight to Istanbul, where she could change for Paris.

Yasin, who had not long before dragged her across the marble floor by her loveliest silk chiffon dupatta, and struck her across the face with the back of his hand, smashing her lip, now bowed before his mother. He said that after her behaviour she should never come back to Pakistan. And since he doubted whether he would live to be old, or that he would go to the West again, it was, as he put it, goodbye, or '*khuda hafiz*'.

'May Allah protect you, and, never forget this –' his mother said, wagging her finger at him as she was helped into the car, 'Allah is always watching you.'

She could hear him laughing as she closed the window.

The following morning, once more wrapped in her favourite trench coat, she was walking around her adopt-

103

ed city. First she'd go to the market; then, perhaps, she'd go to an exhibition, or look again at La Hune, her favourite bookshop, or the other wonderful little places on the Left Bank where she lived, selling hand-made paper and bizarre knick-knacks. In the afternoon she liked to go to the Tuileries or the Luxembourg for a sorbet, watching the children with their au pairs. There was plenty to see. When her first husband had been alive, she'd been a photographer, selling her pictures to Pakistani papers and magazines, and she knew how to look. It wasn't that Paris looked different now; she had only been in Karachi for a month. But she was full of new words, and would talk about the city differently, when she had the opportunity.

Farhana's husband, Michel, a retired critic and journalist, was, as always at that time of the morning, reading in his study on what she called his charpoy – his daybed – supported by oriental tasselled cushions. He hadn't seen his wife the previous night, and now he didn't get up to greet or kiss her, as if it would take too much physical effort. He didn't say he was glad to have her home. But he did wave, lean forward a little, and say, 'You are back early. What happened to your lip?'

'I'll tell you, darling,' she said. 'I'll tell you everything.'

He did say he was keen to hear her story. Not that she knew how to tell it. It would have to come out as it came.

In the late 90s, Farhana's first husband, an army general who had been educated in America, had been publicly beheaded by the Taliban at the behest of his military colleagues, who thought he had become too pro-American. They believed, in fact, that he was betraying the complicity of the army with the Taliban to their mutual enemy, the Americans. For this reason he was captured and driven to the mountains. After she had been sent a photograph of a hand holding up his head, with a large crowd of cheering local villagers in the background, she had fled. Yasin had refused to join her, but remained on the family's country estate, keeping out of politics.

Farhana went to Paris to stay with a wealthy friend, who advised her never to go home. It would also be a good idea to find a steady man to look after her. Paris was ideal for exiles; once, it had welcomed the stateless. But Farhana would have little money and no status, and the French were notoriously racist, only liking people of colour if they were artists or could play the trumpet. What if they mistook her for an Algerian?

Farhana didn't seem concerned, and went along with others' wishes as if she only wanted a quiet life. Now, looking back, she guessed she had been traumatised, and probably still was.

The good friend did a good thing and found the widower Michel, who was ten years older than her. Now in his mid-seventies, he had retired from regular writing in order to read Balzac, study Trollope in English, and become properly familiar with the history of poetry. He had stuck to his word: he was a reader. His chosen destiny made him happy.

At the time he was seen as a tremendous catch, an opportunity not to be missed. He was widowed, well off, cultured, well connected, with numerous books to his name and a lovely flat off the Rue du Bac, on the Left Bank, full of pictures and theatre memorabilia. Farhana, from a distinguished family, was unused to telling anyone who she was. Now she was often informed that she was lucky. Many Parisian women would have wanted this dry old stick. But it was she, a frightened, declining Pakistani woman then in her mid-fifties, who had grabbed the prize. How? She guessed that because she said so little to him, she seemed more demure and mysterious than the others. She certainly had had no idea what she was doing. Perhaps he had pitied her.

It was indeed the case that Michel knew actors, writers and directors. Many of them were distinguished or even world famous in their own world, and they came for dinner once a month and drank a lot. The talk was always of the latest films and books, of what Sarkozy was, or wasn't, doing. If Farhana wondered what Michel wanted from her, there really was no obscurity. They had never been moved by one another. It was companionship: he liked someone to be there while he talked – an urgent and more or less continuous monologue concerning what was in the newspapers. He liked having someone arrange the film screenings he went to, and the plays he attended, often with her. He liked her to sit with him when he listened to entire symphonies by Brahms or Beethoven, nodding at her instructively during the finer parts. She loved this, as it was an opportunity for her to think about important things.

The friend who arranged the marriage included a warning. 'Until the age of sixty a woman still needs passion. But I suspect, dear girl, that your man will make love like a critic.'

'Without asking for it, one day I ran to the airport and found myself dumped in a completely new life, as a middle-aged immigrant,' said Farhana. 'How would I know how a critic makes love?'

'Watch out,' said her friend. 'Fastidious.'

Farhana and Michel had sex twice: once before the marriage, and once after, which was more than enough for him. The first time he ejaculated immediately, and the second he suffered cramp and howled awfully, followed by a coughing fit which he thought was a heart attack. Farhana suspected the catastrophe might have been caused by her removing his tie. She had never seen him during the day without a tie, and she only saw him at night, wrapped in a dressing gown, if they both had insomnia. She had bought him a cashmere polo-neck one Christmas, but Michel felt his being was an obscenity without a tie, and he never wore casual clothes.

Farhana thought she was done with her homeland; she had been ripped from the past, and the future was comfortable but null. Then, one afternoon, Yasin's wife Nasira, who had escaped him at last to London, insisted on coming to Paris to talk. Now working for a travel agent in Cricklewood, North London, Nasira came from a famous family, and had been a Cleopatra, one of the most striking women of Karachi, who wore the most glamorous saris and shimmering shalwar kameez, with solid gold bangles. Many men had been wild about her, which was, Yasin insisted, part of the problem. Now, in jeans and sweater, she was – apart from the Rolex – as diminished and plain as Farhana realised that she herself was. But these two women, both escapees, liked one another, and had much in common.

Farhana put her fingers under Nasira's chin and raised her face. 'Why have you come to see me here?'

'I must warn you,' Nasira said. Farhana's wild-tempered son, never the most stable of people, was developing into a madman. Out on his country estate in Sind, where he was a feudal landlord, Yasin was, apparently, playing polo aggressively, drinking whisky, copulating brutally, and shooting his many guns at anything alive. And because of the kidnappings, he was trying to import a brand-new armoured BMW with blacked-out windows into the country. His wife believed that, although this tank was extremely heavy and therefore somewhat slow, the 'local

Mr Toad', as she called her husband, would smoke a joint, turn up his favourite Punjabi bhangra music, and soon embrace a tree with the vehicle. Although she despised him, she didn't think another violent death in the family would be good for Farhana.

'What can I do about it?' Farhana asked. 'Are you saying I must go there? I'm too weak now: I can't face it.'

'You can only feel you have done your duty,' her daughter-in-law replied. 'And then live your life – which is what I am doing at last.'

Haltingly, Farhana asked Michel if he would be interested in accompanying her, but he wondered whether it would be dusty, or inconvenient for his stomach. That was the least of it. Still, she made sure to take her first husband's gold watch, cufflinks and fountain pens, which she would deliver to Yasin at last.

On her first afternoon in Paris after the trip, her husband asked her to walk with him. That day there was a wind, and he had his waistcoat on. As always, his hands were behind his back. Leaning forward, he barely lifted his feet from the ground, for fear of falling. 'An old man can come to believe that he could easily be knocked down,' he said. 'If he takes a step—'

Farhana interrupted to say, 'When you return to a country after a terrible shock, and more than a decade away, you will know that the roads will have got wider and the skyscrapers higher. There will be more apartment blocks, more people on the street, new immigrants and tourists coming to see the sights. Michel, I must be ageing because I remember when Karachi was a pleasant post-colonial city.'

'Tell me!'

'The men wore suits and the women dresses. People still read Somerset Maugham, drank gin-and-tonics, and listened to "In the Mood", as if the British had just popped north for the summer. There were flowers in the centre of the road. You could get *The Times* at your club. This time I saw rubble everywhere, a gun every ten yards, high walls and barbed wire. The women outside were afraid, and covered themselves to avoid harassment. A city in lockdown, a war zone after a war. A state of petrifaction. Decline and decay everywhere.'

Yasin had returned from his estate to welcome his mother. During the brief period he was sober, after he woke up around lunchtime and his servant went in to cut his toenails and shave him, Farhana went to his room. Although he had put on weight, and his body was flabby, his head was also shaven now, making him look thuggish.

Visas to the West were almost impossible to obtain these days; terrorism had rendered Pakistanis pariahs. All the same, Farhana wanted to persuade Yasin, before he destroyed his health, to do his best to escape to the West or even, since times were hard, to Australia or New

Zealand, if he could bear it.

He laughed and replied, 'There is no doubt that we have made a mess of things here. We all love to declare our devotion to the country, but apart from Imran Khan, every single one of us, if offered a visa, would pack hurriedly and rush to the exit tomorrow. But, I am sorry, Mother, I will not be joining the others at the border, humbly begging to be let into the land of plenty and reason. Being "tolerated" is the last thing I want.'

'Darling, please, give me one good reason for you not to start a new life.'

'It is here that the reality of the world is lived out.'

The last time he was in France, with his then wife, Yasin said he saw a sign saying 'Disneyland Paris' and laughed so much he wished, for the only time, that his father was also around to appreciate it. He had come to dislike the West more as he got older, and had developed a particular animus against the authority of the EU, which he seemed to believe was run by Dominique Strauss-Kahn. He said not only was the EU hypocritical, but Europe was 'risk-free and easy'. Everything was polite and over-careful in its 'multiculturalism and love for homosexuals'. The brutality was now exported, and the only victims today were Muslims, whom the West had never given up believing were lesser beings.

He said, 'Our family sacrificed good lives in India to ruin this new country. As you know, we are a wild and self-destructive people who live carelessly. Life is cheap, only alcohol is expensive. Think how direct we are: all the hotels have been attacked with suicide bombs. When I walk out onto the street I like to know the chances are I will be shot at. What other country in the world would hide Osama Bin Laden in the centre of a city while pocketing vast amounts of American money to finance the search for him? Mother, you must agree it takes perverse genius of the highest order to walk through that looking glass.'

'It's not comfortable to be so stressed.'

'You stress us, with your drone bombings of civilians.' He asked, 'How is your husband, the man who replaced my father? Do you like him? I can see from your lack of expression that you really don't mind, but you did hurry into his arms very quickly.'

'Forgive me, but I was half-dead and stunned. I'm diabetic, and was diagnosed with extreme anxiety. Day by day I sewed my life back together. Michel gets up in the morning with purpose. You lie there like a teenager.'

'Even if that man's work is pointless?'

'He writes about plays.'

'But what would *Hay Fever* mean here?'

'He respects himself. You say you are religious, but you wallow in cynicism. Didn't you say, in this country the educated have no religion, and the religious have no education?'

'I am not religious,' he said. 'But I am a Muslim.'

'Yasin, it is this country which has corrupted your imagination. Your father wasn't like this. He kept saying that without many voices, including the Christian, devotion to one religion will make us autocrats.'

'Then the fool was begging to be murdered. He would have handed over the country to Jews, colonialists and those who want to bomb us into fundamentalist capitalism. Who here doesn't think that Osama taught those arrogant imperialists a good lesson?' He laughed. 'But are we really to discuss this, Gertrude, Mother?'

'You are too old to play Hamlet.'

There were no theatres, bars or new restaurants in Karachi, and people went to one another's houses. At first she accompanied her son on his nightly round of parties. It was an opportunity for her to see the people she'd grown up with, and for them all to notice how much they had aged.

She kept thinking she had been too long in Paris, for the houses she visited looked dusty, run-down and out-of-date, as if they weren't worth the expense of renovation. Soon she realised that anyone with money, intelligence, education or talent had left, and that the rest were urging their children to escape. They sold their jewellery and ushered them towards the border, saying, 'Get out and never return.' Her friends' children had joined an international class of wealthy but dispossessed people with

American accents who now lived in Beijing, Prague or Toronto, working in hospitals or for law firms or banks. Those left behind were the aged, infirm and hopeless, or those with too many dependants.

At the parties there'd be small talk followed by ferocious drinking. It had been a long time since she'd seen people so shamelessly drunk they were lying under tables. Amongst the drunkest would be Yasin, whom she'd help home at four in the morning. In order to gain entry into the house, he made the servants remain awake until he returned. He would either fall asleep then, or demand a woman, and she found herself fighting with him over the age of the servant girls he took. Fourteen, she said, was too young. Soon she stopped accompanying him, and stayed in the house.

There was nothing to do. She began to sit at the ping-pong table in the living room and write about her life, sometimes by candlelight, since the electricity failed at least twice a day. At least the cook and the servant girl took her seriously, creeping in with big smiles, and kebabs, onion bhajis and mango lassi on a tray, while the sweepress with orange teeth, crouching unnoticed for hours, flicked at the dust across the room. In exchange, Farhana made sure to give them little gifts, shawls, underwear, sandals and loose change.

It was three weeks into the month-long visit that, one afternoon, as she wrote, Yasin came into the room yelling, waving his pistol and saying his father's legacy of watch, pens and cufflinks had been stolen, and he was having the house searched.

'I expect you just threw it all in a drawer, Yasin. Look again.'

'They are happening all the time, these thefts. The people are poorer than you can conceive, Mother. But the cook is particularly naughty. My eye has been on him since I noticed he dyed his beard. He has been filling the fridge with meals no human being has the capacity to eat – I suspect he is feeling guilty. He is our George Clooney – the male kingpin – and the neighbourhood servant girls are in and out of the kitchen, a place I never enter, as you know. Being a kind man, I pay for the abortions on a "three-strikes-and-you're-out" basis. After that, the girls are sent to their village, where they are reviled, persecuted and sometimes killed for their shame. Since I'm not a hundred per cent certain it is that exact bastard, I will follow the correct procedures . . .'

'Good, thank you. Now put the gun away, you're frightening me.'

She was reassured, in a place where, increasingly, she realised no reassurance was possible. Her closest friend, an English teacher whom she'd been at school with, was kidnapped while driving to meet Farhana. Her car was sandwiched between two other cars until it could only come to a stop; her driver had been dragged out at gunpoint, beaten and thrown into a ditch. The woman was blindfolded and taken to a house which, when she could see, resembled a waiting room. At least twenty other kidnapees sat on the floor, waiting for their families to provide money, while other victims were brought in.

That afternoon, when Farhana walked around Paris with her husband, she said, 'My friend has always taught English literature, but more recently wanted to add a post-colonial module so the students might glimpse themselves in an artist's words. But there was a void in the curriculum because she cannot teach Rushdie, or even mention his name. She went into a shop to buy *Midnight's Children*, and the owner shouted, "Get out – how dare you mention these hush-hush matters! You can look at pictures of men having sex with camels, or with children or babies. You can call for the death of the apostate. But promote that writer and this place will be ashes – Mullah Omar said this in 2005! Why can't you read P. G. Wodehouse like everyone else!"'

Farhana's husband, when he heard this, said, 'I am reminded that I saw Milan Kundera the other morning, across the street. He walks to his office every day at the same time. I stop and bow respectfully as he passes. Of course, he pretends not to notice me.'

'He doesn't notice you,' she giggled. 'Why should he notice every old man who stops on the street?'

'I know he notices me. As I say, he prefers not to look up since he is thinking creatively.' He went on, 'At the beginning of *The Book of Laughter and Forgetting*, if I remember correctly, a Czech politician, Clementis, soon to be accused of treason and hanged, is erased from a photograph, leaving only the hat he passed to Gottwald on the day. They are doing the same in your country.'

'They despair, and cling to the old certainties because they think the writer tears them apart.'

'Though it is unbearable, they should be grateful, since he has done them the favour of speaking their disloyalty. The artist chews and digests the world for us, and then presents us with evidence of our humanity. What stands between us and barbarism?'

'Your tie.'

'Apart from my tie, Farhana, there is the complexity of literature. If they cannot see that, they are lacking in the civilisation you see around you. Anyone here could tell you that extreme religion can only create sacrilege and perversion – like Catholic France producing the Marquis de Sade.'

'Please, you go too far, Michel.'

'But how is the boy?'

'The conditions in which he lives have put a jinn inside him.'

'What a massive human effort it must have been to make such a wasteland!'

'And you cannot go onto the street without seeing people carrying rifles and machine guns. When I look around here – at this city – at the people walking peacefully, and the hundreds of years of accumulated achievement, I wonder how it's done.'

'Thank God you have seen that, Farhana. I never thought you noticed where you were. What you describe is not achieved by driving out the Jews, Hindus, Catholics, and anyone who adds to the character and creativity of a city, until you have a monotonous monoculturalism – a new puritanism. If you let the pleasure-haters do that, there will be nothing living.' He stood and looked around at the city as if he had built it himself. 'The careful preservation of the past is the basis of culture. After the Second World War we learned how destructiveness stalks us, and how fragile civil society is.'

She said, 'Everywhere around the world the young are rising up, but in Pakistan they are going to the airport. I've never before been to a place without hope, nor anywhere without one beautiful thing in it, apart from the orchids in my son's garden.'

Michel said, 'This door – to the West – is shut now. In here it is an exclusive spa. Farhana, we are glad to have you, provided you respect our liberality.'

'I do!'

'Count yourself lucky to have slipped inside.'

'Thank you for reminding me, husband.'

'Now tell me, how is it you made such a boy?'

'I will think about that – in my writing.'

'Writing, did you say? Farhana – no!'

Yasin had the house searched several times. 'It's gone,' he said at last. 'We can't find any of it. The only things Father left me. I want you to know, Mother, that I let my servants eat meat, which is like caviar to them. I give them food which is not rotten. And of course they steal from me, and only rarely, when I am really wild, do I whip them. They would never be treated so well else-where, and this is how they reward me.'

'It is mislaid, please, believe me,' she said. 'I have come here and seen that you are a victim awaiting a murderer. Please look more – behind the sofa, for instance – before you follow the procedures.'

She called it work now, her writing. Hadn't her life been more interesting than most? An arresting opening had occurred to her: she would begin with her two hus-bands, and compare Parisian men, their world and meth-ods of love, to that of the men of Pakistan.

She began to get down to it as soon as she woke up, hunched over the ping-pong table, with some rotis on a plate and two standing fans turned full on. It was the only time Farhana felt content and safe in this country, and she had begun this work away from Paris since she knew that, far from encouraging her, Michel would condemn her work as 'a waste of effort'. It was his job to condemn the bad stuff. 'Even before it is written?' she enquired, when discussing the idea with him. 'That would be confinement – and premature.'

Now she said, 'I feel as if I have had two men, you and my son, chattering and bullying me in the ear.'

'Bullying?'

'Don't you see you are beginning to operate more like a big fat censor than a critic. I will resist you,' she said. 'I will even mention to your friends and perhaps to the concierge that I am writing! How the filthy foreign woman stains the quartier with her amateur words!'

'Please. Not that.'

'If you don't announce it to them next time at dinner, there will be a fuss. Look at my cut lip – there is evidence.'

She saw, when she said this, that he was afraid; she might stand up to him and, in time, gain an advantage.

One evening in Karachi she returned from a visit to her friend to find the gates locked. The guard, who sat on a chair outside with his rifle, didn't come to her car. Instead her driver had to get out of their vehicle to let her into the house. Inside, it was silent, and it was never silent: there were more staff than family.

She called her son. 'Where is everyone?'

'I've had enough. I'm following the procedures.'

'What procedures?'

'I set a deadline for the return of my possessions but they were not recovered. I ordered the police to take everyone away. You will see how soon, inshallah, my belongings will come back.'

'How?'

'It is tragic, Mother, but you and I will have to get our own food tonight. The servants are hanging upside down on meat hooks in the police station. They will be there for a few hours, in their own urine and faeces, until they begin to feel uncomfortable. Meanwhile, I am waiting for the Security Expert to become available.'

'Security Expert? What is that?'

'The torturer. This service has now been privatised. We are following your example in the West. He is available by the hour, and I will tip him if the result is positive. What is a fingernail here or there? This is not Downton Abbey. Let's say it is more like your Guantanamo.'

'No, Yasin.'

'Mother, you will see how efficiently we can do things, after your determination to find nothing good in this ravishing country.'

The bell rang. Before she went to her room to think, Farhana saw Yasin and the torturer taking whisky in the living room. She pictured the servants, with whom she'd been friendly – asking for their stories – in the police station.

When she heard the car start in the yard, and the two men got up and went outside, blood and fury rose to her head, and she went to her son before he drove away.

'I am outraged by this. You must not do it. I forbid it absolutely.'

'You don't live here.'

'I said I forbid it.'

'Excuse me.'

'I do not excuse you. He can tear my body instead.' She turned to the torturer. 'Open your bag and start on me! Tear out my heart, bastard! It was me who stole the things! Okay? I don't care if I live or die!' She began to expose her upper body. 'Begin here!'

'You're making a fool of yourself, Mother. Leave the man alone. I have paid him and can't afford to waste money.'

'I attacked Yasin then,' she said to Michel. 'I went for his eyes with my nails, I was so outraged by what he had become. Then I ran into my room, took the sheet from the bed, tied one end around my neck and threw the other over the propellers of the fan. I was beginning to die when they came in. They chased me, and Yasin pulled me across the floor. I was screaming so much, it was a nightmare for them. He struck me, but still I insisted he bring the servants back.'

'And did he?' asked Michel.

'Later I saw them come in, a bedraggled bunch, the women weeping and the sweepress with a broken arm and bleeding head, as Yasin got me into the car and sent me away.'

'You did a good thing, my dear.'

She took his arm. Her husband, walking beside her, looked at the lighted cafes, the churches and the shops, and hummed a song.

She said, 'I want to believe that people can make good lives and can even be happy, despite what has happened to them and the burdens they have to bear.'

'Yes,' he said. 'It would be a good idea to believe that.'

These Mysterious Strangers:
The New Story of the Immigrant

The immigrant has become a contemporary passion in Europe, the vacant point around which ideals clash. Easily available as a token, existing everywhere and nowhere, he is talked about constantly. But in the current public conversation, this figure has not only migrated from one country to another, he has migrated from reality to the collective imagination, where he has been transformed into a terrible fiction.

Whether he or she – and I will call the immigrant he, while being aware that he is stripped of colour, gender and character – the immigrant has been made into something resembling an alien. He is an example of the undead, who will invade, colonise and contaminate, a figure we can never quite digest or vomit. If the twentieth century was replete with uncanny, semi-fictional figures who invaded the decent, upright and hard-working – the pure – this character is re-haunting us in the guise of the immigrant. He is both a familiar, insidious figure, and a new edition of an old idea expressed with refreshed and forceful rhetoric.

Unlike other monsters, the foreign body of the immigrant is unslayable. Resembling a zombie in a video game, he is impossible to kill or finally eliminate not only because he is already silent and dead, but also because there are waves of other similar immigrants just over the border coming right at you. Forgetting that it is unworkable notions of the 'normal' – the fascist normal – which make the usual seem weird, we like to believe that there was a better time when the world didn't shift so much and everything appeared more permanent. We were all alike and comprehensible to one another, and these spectres didn't forever seethe at the windows. Now there seems to be general agreement that all this global movement could be a catastrophe, since these omnivorous figures will eat us alive. From this point of view, the immigrant is eternal: unless we act, he will forever be a source of contagion and horror.

It is impossible to speak up for the immigrant or, more importantly, hear him speak for himself, since everyone, including the most reasonable and sensitive, has made up their mind that the immigrant is everywhere now, and he is too much of a problem. There is, of course, always good reason to be suspicious of agreement: there is nothing more coercive and stupid than consensus, and it is through consensus that inequality is concealed.

Nevertheless, the immigrant is easily dismissed and denigrated since he is now no longer a person. The recently arrived immigrant, the last through the door, and now settling down in the new country, can himself be disgusted by the idea of this newer arrival or interloper, the one who could take his place, because this threatening other does not resemble him in any way. The migrant has no face, no status, no protection and no story. His single identity is to be discussed within the limited rules of the community.

Too superstitious, ambitious, worthless and strange – deposited outside the firmament of the acceptable – the migrant is degraded to the status of an object about whom anything can be said and to whom anything can be done. One thing is certain about him: he will not only rob you of your wealth and social position, he will be monstrous and obscene in his pleasures. These jouissances, it goes without saying, he has obtained at your expense, even as he is subjugated as your slave.

As an idea, then, this concept of the immigrant is familiar, and the usual clichés – the confining power of negative description – apply, as they always have done to those shadows who haunt the in-between or border zones. The immigrant will be inbred, suffer from sexual incontinence and mental illness, and will be both needy and greedy. But in this particular form the immigrant is also a relatively recent creation. Since we depend so much on that which we hate the most, the worse the economy, the more the need for the immigrant – even in a time when we like to compliment ourselves on our relative tolerance.

Women, gays, the disabled and other former margin-
als might, after some struggle, have been afforded dignity, a voice and a place. Yet diversity and multiculturalism
can become forms of exoticism and self-idealisation, and
exaggerations of difference new types of conceit. Meanwhile, a necessary level of hatred is kept going with regard
to the reviled figure of the immigrant. Integration can
never continue; there has to be someone shoved off the
map. Today it will be him, and tomorrow someone else:
the circulation of bodies is determined by profit. The rich
buy freedom; they can always go where they like, while
the poor are not welcome anywhere. But, all the time, by
some perverse magical alchemy, those we need, exploit
and persecute the most are turned into our persecutors.

Others only have the power we give them. The immigrant is a collective hallucination forged in our own
minds. This ever-developing notion, like God or the
devil, is an important creation, being part of ourselves,
but the paranoiac, looking wildly around, can never see
that the foreign body is inside him. Of course not: when
the world is divided so definitively into the Hollywood
binary of good and bad, no one can think clearly. Hate
skews reality even more than love. If the limits of the
world are made by language, we need better words for
all this. The idea of the immigrant creates anxiety only
because he is unknown and has to be kept that way.

This group fantasy and prison of cliché – a base use of

the imagination – reduces the world to a Gothic tale in which there is only the violence of exclusion, and nothing can be thought or done. If it could be, the stranger, with a mixture of naivety and knowing, might be in a position to tell us the truth about ourselves, since he sees more than we know.

The Woman Who Fainted

Luca said goodbye to the party host; he left the alcohol and his friends, took a last look back, almost waved, as if he were going into permanent exile, and went to find his coat with relief, but not without regret. Many of the most important people in his life – some he had known since he was eighteen and worked for a small theatre magazine – were laughing and drinking on comfortable sofas in that large room hung with modern paintings. Others were talking and smoking outside, on the balmy balcony overlooking the city. As it was a seventieth birthday party, a few of his friends had their grown-up children and even their grandchildren with them. Most of the people there, he thought, he would never see again.

But what more was there to say to such a group of successful actors, writers, directors, producers, designers, other critics? A number of acquaintances, knowing he had left regular employment more than five years ago, had asked what he was doing now. Earlier that evening, as he'd strolled to the party, Luca had worked out his story, replying to enquiries, 'working, writing, thinking . . .' It was easy to say, and soon his interlocutors were talking about themselves. What had disturbed him was that at least three people had failed to recognise him, not out of cruelty or even short-sightedness. It was worse than that: they had no idea who he was. He had made a simple mistake, one he swore he would never make again – he had aged.

The small cloakroom near the front door was almost dark except for a side light, and the pile of coats was considerable. Naturally, most of the coats were black. How would he find his own worn jacket? He began on the procedure of picking up each one, putting it to his eyes to examine the label, before dropping it to one side. It took a lot of time, but what was his time for, now?

He wasn't keen to go home. He was a little drunk and the sight of his friends that evening had made him aware that he could do with some time to think about his future, such as it was. He would walk for a while; he loved to see the city at night in silence and semi-darkness, when the people didn't obscure the buildings.

Outside the apartment, when the door to the small lift opened, he was surprised to see that it already contained a red-haired woman in her late thirties. Since they were on the top floor and she was bundled shivering into the corner holding her coat tightly around her, he assumed she'd been unable to get out at the ground floor. Perhaps she had been going up and down for some time.

'Are you okay?' he said, stepping in and pressing the button. 'Are you frightened?' She nodded. 'Did you drink too much?'

She said, 'I might have.'

'Do you have any water?' She shook her head. 'I do – here. I'm Luca Frascati.' She mumbled something. He cupped his ear and said, 'Frida Scolari did you say?'

'Yes.' He looked at her face more closely. She shielded her face. 'Stop! Why are you staring at me like that?'

'Is your mother Cristina?' She nodded. He asked, 'Is she alive?'

'I hope so. Did you hear otherwise?'

'No. I'm just so relieved and glad to hear it,' he said. 'Thank God, and thank you.'

'She lives in Paris.'

'She is fortunate, and a dear woman. She and I were close before you were born. And then . . . She was very – Well, I can't say now . . . Frida!'

He saw that Frida was leaning her head back, her cheek on the mirrored glass of the wall. She had fainted; her knees were buckling, there was nothing for her to hold on to: she would fall.

Fortunately the lift bumped and stopped. He could now take her around the waist and, by one arm, pull her out, depositing her on a chair in the hall. He stood beside her as she sat there, lowering her head between her knees. When she sat up he passed her his bottle of water.

'I agree with your faint. It was traumatic in there,' he said. 'Colleagues, lovers, friends, enemies – they were all present, ageing, stumbling about, showing off, gasping for breath. I had to get out when I felt I was attending my own wake.' She was flapping at her face with her hands. 'Frida,' he said, 'I knew both your parents. You are the best thing to come out of that untidy commotion – of the party, I mean to say. Can I get you a taxi?'

She nodded and he hurried out into the street. The cab he found waited outside while he helped Frida out of the apartment block. In the taxi he sat close to her, to stop her swaying. She smelled of perfume and marijuana, and he was afraid she might be sick. When the cab stopped, fifteen minutes' drive away, she continued to sit there, slumped. He paid the driver, went round and opened her door, and helped her into her building. He knew it would be difficult work getting her up the stairs, and he went behind her, in case she fell backwards. He did that, and she gave him her keys. While he fumbled with them, she thought it would be a good idea to sit on the ground. As he was in his late sixties it was quite an experience to get her to stand up. At last he opened the door and helped her in.

Her bed was wide; it was in the centre of the room, under a skylight which, he guessed, lying there, she liked to look through. But the room was small, and its shelves were packed with books and CDs. To one side there was a stove, a separate bathroom and, he thought, another small room, perhaps a study.

She lay down on the bed and seemed comfortable when he pulled a blanket over her. Though she was twitching a little, her eyes were closed; he thought she'd soon be asleep. It was disappointing, but he'd leave her his phone number and walk home.

He had turned away when she said, 'I won't be able to sleep. And I'm afraid I'll disappear. There's a bottle of vodka over there. Pour me some, please.' She reached out to him, 'Do you have something else to do now?'

'Me? No. Nothing. It's late. All I look forward to, before sleeping, is a book.'

'The room is revolving, rather. If you left too soon, I'd be worried.' She was now clutching at her mattress with outstretched arms. 'I might go mad. I'm so grateful. You're sweet. Are you as kind to everyone?'

'If they need me. But it's you – you, Frida! I'm totally surprised and delighted.'

She said, 'Luca, if you're so nice, will you please say something – to help keep me grounded?'

'Yes, of course. You might find it hard to believe,' he said, pulling up a chair and sitting down not far from her, 'but there was a time when people were afraid of me. A couple of my sentences could knock you almost dead.'

'But why? What did you do?'

'I was a critic, you know. For ten years I was feared and

powerful – until I was replaced by a younger man. The usual story. For the last twelve years I have taught a little, written a bit, and lived on more or less nothing. I wrote two books, one about the British writer Edward Bond, which no one read, and a lovely monograph on darkness in Visconti, which no one published. I will bring it to you tomorrow, if you want. As for my book on Beckett . . . You know I met him several times?'

There was a pause while Luca found two glasses and put the vodka on the table next to her. He poured for them both before sitting down again. He sipped the neat vodka and said, 'An out-of-work critic is regarded rather like a myopic sniper: he can finally be hated for his necessary work. I noticed that people are still afraid to approach me. Or they won't forget some long-ago grudge.' There was a silence and he watched her move about restlessly, as if she were trying to refocus everything. He said, 'Would it be okay if you told me a little about your mother?'

'What for?'

'I'd be most grateful for any news.'

'I'll only tell you this.' She sat up, looked about wildly, lay down again, and said, 'Her husband the diplomat died two years ago.'

'I heard. I'm sure she is still quite a catch. She was beautiful. If only I could see her. Before I go to sleep I think of her often. What does she do?'

'She loves to eat and think about clothes, and read. And she—'

'I like that. You make it sound as if she has no worries at all. You must give me her email address.'

'One day – when I feel better.'

'Does she ever mention me – Luca, Luca Frascati?'

Frida said, 'I was taken to the party by a friend of my mother's. I recognised people, but I don't know them. Stupidly, I smoked something on the balcony, thinking it might make me laugh and approach people and join in more. It was too strong. My legs dissolved and my mind started turning over and over, and flashing like a shutter. It still is.' She giggled. 'But I can see pretty things.' She sat up suddenly and said, 'Anyway, why are you thinking of my mother? Tell me, what is your situation tonight? What would your wife say if she knew you were here with me?'

'What wife? Oh, Frida, I am living in the apartment of a ramshackle mad-haired woman I was together with for a month, years ago. She makes my flesh crawl and we never speak except to abuse one another. But I have a tiny pension, and sometimes I help a friend sell cheese in the market. The woman likes me to help with the bills, go shopping, and walk her dogs. She has had cancer of the liver for some time. Most of it has been removed, but it returns, as these things do. When she dies, her children will reclaim the house and I will have to leave. But where?

I have nothing of my own. I could die alone. If you can believe it, we were a generation who didn't believe in money, and, to be honest, I didn't think I'd get to be this age.'

'You thought you'd just die?'

'Or be excused, somehow. Yes, you're laughing. I should have laughed then, when I thought I had integrity. Beneath most people, you know – and this I've noticed recently – there is always an abyss, covered over with leaves and branches. But one day your foot goes through it, and you see you are one fatal step from eternity, a blink away from destitution . . .'

She shouted suddenly, 'What the fuck is that?'

He stood up and looked around. 'What? My eyesight is poor – is it an animal?'

'Is that yours?'

'Frida, what is it?'

'Look – there, there! You've put a hat on a bed! Are you kamikaze – that could kill us instantly.'

He snatched up his hat, put it on a table and smoothed it down. 'Sorry, so sorry,' he said.

She relaxed. 'Don't you know me either, Luca? I'm sure you saw me. I was an actress for years. I appeared in this and that for no money and didn't get anywhere. But you look at me blankly. Oh dear. My mother also thought I was ridiculous and she gave me advice.'

'What did the dear woman say? She was always promiscuous, if you don't mind me saying, with her advice.'

Frida said, 'Even now, she said, women are defined by their men. She said I should marry a rich one while I still had the breasts for it.'

'Did she like your breasts?'

'She complimented them, and was jealous.' She giggled. 'I think it was because I said I'd inherited them from my father.'

He said, 'Did she take her own advice?' There was a pause. 'Frida?' he said again.

She seemed to have fallen into a stupor. He sat there quietly for a bit, before getting up and taking a few steps into the other little room. He saw a couch, covered in clothes, and a little desk, piled with books and clothes. He caught a sudden movement in the room and was startled. It was himself in a mirror, a harried, almost haunted and probably mad old man in need of a haircut. When had he grown so plump? Looking away, he noticed there were some photographs in a pile; he picked them up, and was beginning to look through them when he heard her voice.

'Naturally, she didn't think for a moment of taking her own advice,' she was saying. 'Who does? I remember she was completely preoccupied and mad for the grand diplomat. She batted his wife right out of the way until the poor woman went crazy. Mother wanted to travel and live here and there, and look at this and that, and photograph people in mud huts. And she did – at his expense.'

He came in and sat down again. 'What was your rich man like?'

She laughed. 'He had an accountancy firm, can you imagine. He was dull and he didn't like to part with money. I wasn't even sure he was a breast man, after all. To my credit, Luca, I scared the shit out of him. Often, at night, I wake up around three, you know. I hate that hour but am usually around to see it. And I'd be screaming, terrified that I was being chased by an axeman. He'd jump right out of bed and leave the room. Then he left the country. He wanted a woman to admire him, he wasn't interested in being a saint or a psychiatrist. Soon he'd had enough. I was back on my own.'

Luca leaned forward in his chair. 'But why would you wake up screaming like that, dear girl? What has happened to you?'

She was sitting up now, and fumbling in a side drawer. She began to roll a joint.

He went on, 'Your father I remember well. I was just finishing with your mother when he came on the scene. He was big then with huge black hair and manic energy, drinking, smoking, sweating, spitting everywhere, addressing massive student meetings, making speeches, running his paper. I must have some copies at home.

'Frida, look at me, please. Don't you remember me at all?' Luca said. 'Your parents eventually lived together in a big communal house, and I was upstairs. We sat around night after night discussing society, revolution and the family, and your dad said we should share the children around. Of course, this was a way for him to do nothing himself. You were supposed to be communal property, and we would bring you up together – all of us, friends, comrades, sisters. That's what we believed then. We dismiss the fundamentalists of today, but it makes me laugh even more to think I was once a Maoist – one who always had to confess he loved the highest art!' He leaned towards her and said confidentially, 'As I get older, my contempt for all that increases. Don't be offended – I only mean contempt for what we were. Your father wanted us to support the Cultural Revolution.'

'And did you?'

'Yes, kill the bourgeoisie – the bourgeoisie who were our own parents! We were authoritarian in the name of liberty! Before the anarchy of paradise there would be discipline! The sheer stupidity was absurd. Shelley calls it "serious folly".

'Cristina preferred your father to me. He had certainty and strong desire. He was a rabble-rouser and, as you know, the rabble are easily aroused. Look at me, I lack confidence, I'm terrified of the slightest thing. I was only a liberal critic, and so I let her go. You can only catch the other by the libido. And for reasons I forget, I didn't believe you could make claims on people.'

'So – what happened? Where did you go?'

'The commune broke up and we dispersed to different places in the neighbourhood. Did you know that for two years, because I worked in the evenings, I looked after you as a child, while your mother worked as a journalist and your dad was doing more important things? I took you to school on my shoulders, we went to the park, we played together for hours, and I fed and bathed you at my place. There must be photographs of us together somewhere.' He sat quietly for a moment. 'I remember when you wanted a watch. I couldn't say no to you. We went to a shop and spent all my money on it. Then you went back to your parents. You wanted them.

'But your dad had a lot of women around, as radical political figures tend to, you probably know that. Then they both moved away. I was dumped, as if my relationship with you had been nothing. I believed in it; I'd helped bring you up. I was ready to be a parent.

'You've forgotten me. It's all gone. There's no reason why you would remember.' He got up and fetched her an ashtray. She offered him the joint but he shook his head. He poured himself another drink. 'Perhaps I should go.'

'Will you go back to the party? There'll be alcohol there.'

'Some of those people I absolutely loathe.'

She laughed. 'But you said they're your friends.'

'They are my only friends, though I never see them now.'

'You must envy them.'

'Dear girl, at times tonight I was almost levitating with envy as I contemplated their houses, their furniture, their country places. Some of them made millions from the theatre and cinema – they had taken such good care of themselves.' He was silent, before saying, 'Do you have that address?'

She drew on her joint. 'Sorry, what are you talking about?'

'Your mother. I am available to go to Paris to visit her. Perhaps this weekend—'

Frida said, 'You're not in touch with her, yet you still like her that much?'

'I knew her for a long time – and I was with her for two years, on and off. I took her to the theatre and movies when I received tickets. She began to love the opera. She had always been political, of course, and she had a lot of nerve. One night, I was watching TV, and suddenly she blazed onto some show or other, arguing with a revered church father, giving him a roasting which must have reminded him of a premature hell.'

'She's quieter now.'

'Naturally. I made her cultured when she became bored by the vapid political struggle and the hippy Marxism. She wanted to grow up, read women writers and think for herself. I gave her books – I made her subtle.'

'Subtle! If she actually came into the room now, you'd be terrified.'

'Why do you say that?'

'She would swing about grandly, looking at everything, and ask, "What do you actually have to offer now, Luca?"'

Frida poured herself another drink. He shook his head. 'I remember her as more humble. Cristina said to me, "I'll never know anything, Luca." But I watched her grow, Frida.'

'With or without you, she was certainly intending to grow, Luca,' said Frida. 'My father died and my sister and I had to settle down and adore her, always telling her how magnificent and competent she was. From her side, she thought we should just get up and get on with things. Why would we not become successful people? She was capable of great love – with a man. She believes she deserves everything. I dream she is a tower, or sometimes a giraffe, looking down on ugly us. She crushed us without knowing it. By the time I was fourteen I wasn't living at home . . .' She went on, 'After the diplomat died Mother grew sick of galleries and lunches with the other less-than-merry widows. She began to go to Africa or Asia or Eastern Europe to write reports on raped women. She is even more irreproachable now.'

'But I can still talk a little,' he said.

'The last thing she wants to hear about are the old days.'

He poured himself the rest of the vodka, dropped the bottle in the bin and said, 'She knows how much I know. She respected my ideas.'

'What ideas?'

'About theatre.'

'They'll be out of date.'

He said, 'My humour will get through to her.'

There was a silence. He noticed Frida was looking at him. 'What is it?'

'I've been observing you.'

'You must be feeling better, my dear.'

'But are you?'

'What do you mean?'

'You're biting your nails and making faces. Your body won't keep still. Try now – try and be static.'

'Surely I am tranquil. I'm almost a dead man.'

'Now, look – your knee's jiggling.'

'To hell with my knee, I'm bored,' he said. He stood up abruptly and sat down again. 'I wake up bored. It's unbearable to have no place or point anywhere. Boredom is my cancer; it's killing me. "He died of boredom" – scrawl it on my gravestone.'

'Let me tell you something, Luca,' she said. 'Your anger is preventing you thinking what to do. You should meditate.'

'I must? Do not mock me,' he said. 'Haven't I tried to be kind tonight?'

'You must meet me on Friday morning at nine. I will give you a free lesson. When you realise you enjoy it, you can sign on with me. Meditation helps with difficult things like anxiety and fear. Believe me, you will feel calm.'

'How can it be a solution to sit and do nothing? I already do that! Your mother would never recommend anything so ridiculous. She was full of ideas.'

'Remember, I am not a telephone to her. I was always a bigger fan of my father's suicidal extremity.'

'You were?'

'Mother rightly called Father "insurrectionary". Don't we need trouble-makers and tribunes of the proletariat? It shows greatness to protect the poor and exploited! You rant and choose to be offended rather than hear me.'

'Hear your nonsense?' He got up and gestured at the room. 'Look at this place—'

'What's wrong with it?'

'It's untidy, it's even dirty. There is ash and candle wax here. Your clothes are on the floor, the glasses are dirty and the bins are unemptied. You, from your decent family, can barely care for yourself. And don't you think I'm sick of fatuous ideas? Do you not have the ability to do anything to alleviate your condition?'

'Like give you my mother's email address?'

'I understand now that it is an enviable talent, almost a kind of genius, to find a good partner. You and I – we haven't achieved good marriages. Or even children, and certainly not financial stability. We are just clinging on. This is the new Europe: democracy, religion, culture – it could easily be knocked out again. All of us are on the razor's edge. The country has collapsed. Soon it will be the Muslims or the Chinese who will rule us – anyone who really believes, anyone with a passionate intensity. Your father – he fought, he believed.'

'You look anguished.'

'He had an authoritarian state of mind. He was unshakeable. It's commendable and mad. It—'

'Shut up,' she said. 'Just don't bother to say anything about my father . . .'

He opened his mouth. She got up, wobbled a little on her feet, gathered herself together, took a step forward – and slapped him.

After a time he said, 'Will you tell your mother that you struck me?'

'I don't speak to her.' She sat down again. 'I haven't spoken to her for months and won't again until she gets in touch, and who knows when that will be. When the time comes I will ask her about you, yes.' She went on, 'I failed. I failed at my chosen thing. I failed for a long time. Failure was good for me. I found something else. I have begun to teach acting and Shakespeare to school-children.'

'Do they understand it?'

'I'm a pessimistic optimist,' she said. 'I try to give people a vocabulary, a language, to express what they need to say. I love it. I enjoy it more than anything. What do you love? What do you love to do? Really, it's the only question.' She shook her fist. 'My thirties have been a bit shaky. But my forties will be a riot.'

He was still rubbing his face. 'I'll come to the meditation on Friday. I'm sure it will help,' he said. 'Do you use your spare room for the class?'

She opened her drawer and handed him a card. 'No, why do you ask? Here's the address.'

He put it in his pocket. 'Thank you. But tell me, are you renting that spare room?'

'It's hardly a room,' she said. 'You had a good look in there.'

'I could help you with the rent. I've served culture, in my way – I could put your books in alphabetical order. I'll look after you again, Frida,' he said.

'It would be nice to have company. But I think I might get a cat.' She sighed and said, 'Don't worry, Luca, there will be other paradises.'

'Don't be ridiculous, why would there be?'

She stood up and opened the curtains. The light was coming up. He got up and stood beside her. Together they looked into the park opposite.

'They'll be opening the park soon,' she said. 'Will you walk across it? I'll wave to you.'

'Okay,' he said, putting on his hat and coat. 'I'll do that. Goodbye.'

As he walked across the park, he was determined not

to turn and look back because she wouldn't be there to wave. No one was sincere; and, anyway, he couldn't possibly have anything she wanted. But, at the exit, he did stop and turn. He thought he should; it would soon be time to face important things. And she was there because she knew he would turn. She was standing, doing her breathing exercises, he guessed. And before he went away, he waved back.

The Heart of Whiteness

E. R. Braithwaite's *To Sir, With Love*

I didn't know I was coloured until I went to school. It wasn't until much later that I knew what it meant. Books helped me: in Bromley Library in 1970, aged sixteen – around the time I was reading Ian Fleming, the Saint, P. G. Wodehouse, James Baldwin and Mickey Spillane – I found *To Sir, With Love*. As a half-Indian, half-English schoolboy living in the suburbs with no vocabulary for describing his experience, this 1959 novel about a black teacher in Cable Street in London's East End was a revelation. At last there was a way to talk about race and what racism might do to someone. This had barely begun as a public discussion in Britain, except in the negative by people like Enoch Powell, who, in the midst of Britain's imperial decay and decline, were attempting a resurgence of supremacy.

This straightforward and moving story of an educated Guyanese in a new-style 'free' school – a man journeying into whiteness, class, miscegenation and teenage sexuality – helped me see what might be possible for a tyro writer tackling a subject that had hardly been broached by British artists. Growing up in an atmosphere of casual and deliberate racism, forbidden from visiting various houses, and with fascist groups like the British National Party around us in South London, I was beginning to think of how I might approach this material in fiction and begin to write myself out of the corner I was in.

With its reference to Rosa Parks and the early civil rights protests in the US, the novel begins with an insult on a London bus. A woman refuses to sit next to a black man because of his colour. It is a very clear beginning to the story. The woman wants this man to know something. It is not that he is merely dehumanised for her: she could, after all, merely ignore him or, in fact, not see him at all. But she doesn't. He is not 'invisible' as he might once have been. In his essay 'Marrakech' (1939), George Orwell comments, '[I]t is always difficult to believe that you are walking among human beings. All colonial empires are in reality founded upon that fact. The people have brown faces – besides, there are so many of them! [. . .] Are they really the same flesh as yourself? Or are they merely a kind of undifferentiated brown stuff . . . ?'

But now, after the empire, and as London begins to change, the black man is too present, and so the woman becomes coercive. She insists, with her refusal to share a seat with him, that he see himself through her eyes and know his place. The insult not only creates a necessary distance between them – making it clear that he is abhorrent to her – but tells us that she is superior to him and that this gives her the power to hurt. She could traumatise him repeatedly if she wished. At the moment of the insult he no longer has an identity of his own; he exists only as she sees him. She counts for more than he does and, because he is inferior, she can enjoy humiliating him. And we know, as she petrifies him, that she takes pleasure in it.

To Sir, With Love bristles with such humiliations and the attempts of the new teacher, Ricky Braithwaite, to live with them. He has to. He loves the idea of Britain, though Britain doesn't love him as much as he thought it might. Braithwaite has served in the RAF and now, after the war, is desperate for a job. He is a qualified electrical engineer, but because of his colour has been unable to find a position. He has been rejected repeatedly and told that whites will not accept a black man in authority over them.

To Sir, With Love is a shocking novel because the desire to degrade and humiliate is so strong in the whites. Braithwaite has to deal with this constantly. As the only major black character in the book, this is the story of a man trying not to lose his mind while keeping his temper – a daily struggle involving him in such an awful, limiting self-restraint that it is difficult to know whether he is a saint or masochist. He has, unfortunately, to be good all the time for fear of descending into the clichés with which the whites surround him.

The desire to degrade and humiliate is not simply an

addictive sadistic amusement, although there is a great deal of that in this book. It is also the desire to sustain power: the power of whiteness, of whiteness as the norm, the core, the invisible standard of what a person should be in order to become entirely acceptable. This notion of whiteness begins to decline in the early post-war period, as the world starts to come to Britain, altering it forever. But in London, a city devastated by war, the pleasures of privilege and empire were never going to be easy to give up. Hence the desire to defend an already dead idea. The insult, therefore, is unambiguously and structurally supremacist. Blacks, Asians and others will always be secondary in derivation, with no identity of their own. They are like us, but never enough like us. They are separate; they are not authentic, but failures or 'mimic men', bad copies of the original. Their position is always impossible, which is how the whites like it.

Of course, as Ricky Braithwaite points out when teased and goaded to exasperation, there is nothing natural about this notion of whiteness as the supreme standard. It is as arbitrary and socially conditioned as every other moral ideal. The children begin to understand this because to a certain extent Braithwaite – under the descriptions of others – resembles the pupils he is trying to instruct. The immigrant, like the teenager, is gradually losing his home, his past, his safety and stability. Like them, he has been placed outside. He wants to be assimilated, to find a position where he can live a fruitful life, but the whites will not have it, preferring the fantasy of the black or alien intruder. What sustains racial insults might be the wish for unstained whiteness, for purity and a healthy world in which the intrusions of others' gratification don't exist. But there is another sense in which the racist never wants the pleasures of persecution to end.

If blacks are considered, in this branding, to be savages – uncontrolled, greedy, noisy, over-sexualised, dependent and so on – there is a similarity here with the children Braithwaite is teaching. One of Braithwaite's colleagues, Weston, considers his job as 'survival' and the children as barely human. But if a place has been assigned to them, there is always the danger they will escape their fate. Someone, somewhere – women, children, deviants, blacks, colonial subjects – could be getting too excited and will have to be suppressed. As Orwell recognised, as a colonial administrator in Burma, for the ruler the key thing is the maintenance of order and 'the long struggle not to be laughed at'.

However, Alex Florian, the novel's headmaster, likes children and thinks of them as individuals rather than as a mob or horde. He knows how they and their parents suffered in the war and the deprivation they are currently living with. Braithwaite based Florian on Alex Bloom, the headmaster who ran the St George-in-the-East secondary modern school on Cable Street where E. R. Braithwaite himself taught. Bloom wanted to attempt a different way of interacting with children. Influenced by the work of Freud and his followers such as Melanie Klein and the psychoanalyst of children D. W. Winnicott, Bloom wanted to escape the Dickensian model of discipline, obedience and punishment to which English working-class children had long been subjected. Children were humiliated for their own good; nothing was feared more than the collapse of authority, which had to be sustained at all costs. But in the new thinking, new questions arose: what would happen if children didn't represent the uncertainties of the adults? If they were not seen as having monstrous and uncontrollable appetites which had to be subjugated?

In *To Sir, With Love* the teacher Ricky Braithwaite sees that he has to change the children's attitude to him as a black man before he can interact with them positively, before anything good can take place. Fear, submission and hate make only chaos. It's significant that Ricky Braithwaite, despite Greenslade being a progressive school, doesn't introduce more freedom into the situation in which he finds himself. He wants more rules, insisting on politeness and respect, knowing that we are profoundly dependent on the way others speak to us. He asks the children to read, explaining that they are made and constrained by language. This is why jokes and insults matter; no abuse is a trivial 'one-off'. The insult is violent, political and authoritarian, part of a collective view which can be resisted. Poetry, for him, provides better words for things.

To Sir, With Love is partly a record of where we were in Britain at the beginning of the 60s. From this powerful testimony we can see what has changed and how we've remained the same. The language used about strangers and immigrants in the novel is used by fascists and fundamentalists today. Unsurprisingly, we are still people who love to hate, and are much bothered by what we imagine to be others' pleasure. Their happiness is always more than ours; however much joy we might have, we have been cheated, deprived and exploited. We are missing out on something which the other, however poor they are, clearly enjoys. And what could be more intolerable than other people's ecstasy?

The insult, which exposes this envy, excludes exchange. The woman on the bus and many other characters in the novel fear equality. What might happen if people encountered one another directly, without a barrier of subjection or oppression? But it is precisely because equality is unpredictable that it is also difficult and more dangerous than the dreary repetition of degradation. We will never not be ambivalent about others. We do know that worthwhile relationships can happen, and that equality makes difference possible.

Ricky Braithwaite knows he didn't make the difficult world in which he has arrived, but he never gives up resisting its deadness in his own way. He knows he can bring it to life through language. Appearance isn't destiny if we change the way we speak. And we can find ourselves in books, as I did with this one.

We Are the Wide-Eyed Piccaninnies

I was fourteen in 1968 and one of the horrors of my teenage years was Enoch Powell. For a mixed-race kid, this stiff ex-colonial zealot with his obscene, Grand Guignol talk of whips, blood, excreta, urination and wide-eyed piccaninnies was a monstrous, scary bogeyman. I remember his name being whispered by my uncles for fear I would overhear.

I grew up near Biggin Hill airfield in Kent, in the shadow of the Second World War. We walked past bomb sites every day; my grandmother had been a 'fire watcher' and talked about the terror of the nightly Luftwaffe raids. With his stern prophet's nostalgia, bulging eyes and military moustache, Powell reminded us of Hitler, and the pathology of his increasing number of followers soon became as disquieting as his pronouncements. At school, Powell's name soon become one terrifying word – Enoch. As well as being an insult, it began to be used with elation. 'Enoch will deal with you lot,' and, 'Enoch will soon be knocking on your door, pal.' 'Knock, knock, it's Enoch,' people would say as they passed. Neighbours in the London suburbs began to state with some defiance,

'Our family is with Enoch.' More skinheads appeared.

It was said, after Powell mooted the idea of a Ministry of Repatriation, that we 'offspring', as he called the children of immigrants, would be sent away. 'A policy of assisting repatriation by payment of fares and grants is part of the official policy of the Conservative Party,' he stated in 1968. Sometimes, idly, I wondered how I might like it in India or Pakistan, where I'd never been, and whether I'd be welcomed. But others said that if we were born here, as I was, it would be only our parents who would be sent back. We would, then, have to fend for ourselves, and I imagined a parentless pack of us unwanted mongrels, hunting for food in the nearby woods.

Repatriation, Powell said, 'would help to achieve with minimum friction what must surely be the object of everyone – to prevent, so far as that is still possible, a major racial problem in the Britain of AD 2000'. It was clear: if Britain had lost an empire and not yet recovered from the war, our added presence would only cause more strife – homelessness, joblessness, prostitution and drug addiction. Soon the indigenous whites would be a 'persecuted minority' or 'strangers' in their own country. It would be our turn, presumably, to do the persecuting.

Powell, this ghost of the empire, was not just a run-of-the-mill racist. His influence was not negligible; he moved British politics to the right and set the agenda we address today. Politicians attack minorities when they want to impress the public with their toughness as 'truth-tellers'. And Powell's influence extended far. In 1976 – the year of the Clash's 'White Riot' – and eight years after Powell's major speeches, one of my heroes, the great Eric Clapton, ordered an audience to vote for Powell to prevent Britain becoming a 'black colony'. Clapton said that 'Britain should get the wogs out, get the coons out,' before repeatedly shouting the National Front slogan 'Keep Britain White'.

A middle-class, only child from Birmingham, socially inept and repressed, Powell had taken refuge in books and 'scholarship' for most of his life. He was happiest during the war, where he spent three years in military intelligence in India. It was 'intoxicating'. Like a lot of Brits, he loved the empire and colonial India, where he could escape his parents and the constraints of Britain, and spend time with other men. Many Indians were intimidated by and subservient to British soldiers, as my family attested. Like most colonialists, Powell was a bigger, more powerful man in India than he'd have been in England. No wonder he was patriotic and believed that giving up the empire would be a disaster. 'I had always been an imperialist and a Tory,' he said.

On his return in 1945, Powell went into politics. Like the grandees he aspired to be, he took up church-going and fox-hunting. Before his speeches on race, he was an obedient servant of the state, uninteresting, undistinguished and barely known as a politician. But early on, during the post-war consensus, he was, in fact, a proto-Thatcherite: an individualist and anti-union supporter of the free market and lower taxes with a utopian vision of unregulated capitalism in which, miraculously, everything people required would be provided by the simple need for profit. Soon, as Thatcher said, there would be no alternative.

But, in 1968, that great year of newness, experimentation and hope, when people were thinking in new ways about oppression, relationships and equality, there was a terrible return. This odd Edwardian figure popped up into public life, and decided to become a demagogue. Richard Crossman, in his diary of 1968, wrote worriedly of Powell's celebrity appeal to 'mass opinion, right over our parliament and his party leadership'.

Appealing to the worst in people – their hate – is a guaranteed way to get attention, but it is also fatal. Partly because he liked to talk in whole sentences, Powell was called clever, and he was forever translating Herodotus. But he wasn't smart enough to resist the temptation of instant populism, for which he traded in his reputation. Racism is the fool's gold, or, rather, the crack cocaine of politics. The seventies were a dangerous time for people of colour – the National Front was active and violent, particularly in South London, and it was an ignoble sacrifice for Powell to attack the most vulnerable and unprotected, those workers who had left their homes to come to Britain. He elevated his phobia to a political position, and there was no going back. He had convinced himself he had a message for mankind, and it was this unblinking certainty and sadism, rather than its content, which points to his madness.

Like many racists, Powell was nostalgic in his fantasies: before all this mixing, there was a time of clarity and plenitude, when Britishness was fixed and people knew who they were. Powell refused to allow his certainties to come into contact with reality. He had wanted to know India, but barely troubled himself with Britain and, apart from some weekends in Wolverhampton, lived for most of his life in Belgravia.

In contrast to the crude caricatures of people of colour perpetrated by Powell, the Guyanese-born, Cambridge-educated writer E. R. Braithwaite – who served in the RAF before becoming a teacher in the East End because he couldn't get a job as an engineer – writes in detail about race between the late forties and the mid-sixties. Three important works in particular, *To Sir, With Love*, *Reluctant Neighbours* and *Choice of Straws*, deal with this period. If being a person involves recognition from others, here we see the negative. From a clear-eyed, brave novelist we learn about the everyday humiliations, abuse and remarks that people of colour had to face after being invited to help run the NHS and the transport system. To make the future it wanted, Britain needed the best doctors, engineers, architects, artists and workers of all kinds, and it imported them, before insulting them.

Enoch Powell liked to complain about the vile 'imputation and innuendo' made about him. He was keen to be a martyr and victim. Braithwaite, for his part, really suffered. He catalogues the systemic and degrading exclusion from jobs and housing that so disillusioned immigrants with the British and their babble about fairness, liberty and the mother country. Braithwaite describes the rage and hate that relentless humiliation inevitably engenders, as colonialism did, in its time. Powell probably intuited the simple idea that tyranny creates resistance, and grasped that future conflicts would be caused by the tyranny he supported, hence his apocalypticism. Nevertheless, this was not something he had the human ability to understand, even as he had little sense of other people. Denial is the political trope par excellence.

Powell developed his own schoolmasterish look. Always in black, sometimes in a long overcoat and occasionally in a little homburg, he was punky and subversive, and came to enjoy making everyone furious with his perfectly judged provocations delivered at the wrong/ right time. And he had the cheek to call *us* 'a roomful of gunpowder'. He didn't fit in, but he certainly liked to disorientate and traumatise us. After he spoke, we were in freefall; we didn't know where or who we were. Powell wanted to confirm us as outsiders, as unintelligible and unwanted, but this helped us clarify things and created resistance. Out of Eric Clapton's provocative statements, for instance, came Rock Against Racism, created by artists, musicians and activists to combat fascism. Then there was identity politics. We were not nothing; we had histories and, unlike him, we had futures.

Powell was creating the conflict he claimed to be the solution to. In the process he alienated and split his own party. This man who couldn't conceive of, nor bear, the idea of equality soon found himself supported by the National Front. Powell had called himself a Nietzschean as a young man, but Nietzsche would have hated the wretched appeal to the mob or 'herd'. Powell was merely addressing the bitter rabble, and, for so fastidious a man, this would have been distasteful, and he must have considered how incapable our intelligence can be when it comes to protecting us from the temptations of self-destruction.

He cheated his followers, because all he gave them was the brief thrill of superiority and hatred. Nothing substantial altered in the world, and the wild, conscience-less capitalism which developed out of the economic vision he adapted from Hayek created wealth for some, but otherwise had no respect for Powell's followers' homes or jobs, nor for the other things he cared about – tradition, national borders, patriotism or religion. In Enoch's world it would be everyone for themselves; selfishness would benefit everyone.

Although Powell was attacked and condemned by students wherever he went, he didn't trouble himself to think about the profound social changes sweeping the country as young people attempted to liberate themselves from the assumptions of the past. Britain wasn't decaying, it was remaking itself, even as it didn't know how the story would end.

In London now, if you stroll through the crowds on a bright autumn Sunday afternoon near the museums and highly decorated shop fronts, even for those of us who have been here for years, this multiracial metropolis – less frantic than New York, and with more purpose than Paris, and with its scores of languages – seems like nothing which has ever been made before. And it grows ever more busy, bustling and compelling in its beauty, multiplicity and promise, particularly for those of us who remember how dull and eventless London could seem in the seventies, especially on Sundays.

Britain survived Powell and became something he couldn't possibly have envisioned. When it came to human creativity, Powell was without imagination. He really was a pessimist and lacked faith in the ability of people to co-operate with one another, to collaborate and make alliances. The cultural collisions he was afraid of are the affirmative side of globalisation. People do not love one another because they are 'the same', and they don't always kill one another because they are different. Where, indeed, does difference begin? Why would it begin with race or colour?

Racism is the lowest form of snobbery. Its language mutates: not long ago the word 'immigrant' became an insult, a stand-in for 'Paki' or 'nigger'. We remain an obstruction to 'unity', and people like Powell, men of *ressentiment*, with their omens and desire to humiliate, will return repeatedly to divide and create difference. The neo-liberal experiment that began in the eighties uses racism as a vicious entertainment, as a sideshow, while the wealthy continue to accumulate. But we are all migrants from somewhere, and if we remember that, we could all go somewhere – together.

The Land of the Old

What a hubbub! Hush! – I whisper animatedly to the male and female voices in the other room. I cannot hear, and I do not need to be made cantankerous!

In this room where I sit leaning forward on a hard chair, as alert as I'll ever be, it is silent. In there, where my master Raymond lies on his bed, it is busy at the moment. He is working, giving a million instructions to his chattering staff. Meanwhile, I wait, straining to hear his voice. In a moment, when he tires, and it will suddenly occur to him that he could relax, he will blurt out my name and I will hurry to him. The others will leave. Today, perhaps, he will deliver his verdict. I need to hear it. At that moment my future will be decided. The world is complicated, but this question couldn't be simpler.

Will I live or will I die?

If he's at this house, rather than in one of his other properties, the old man usually calls me to his room at around this time. I make sure I am washed, perfumed and prepared. He will be lying on his bed and first I will massage his legs and feet, and then his whole body, particularly his head, which he loves, before offering him

169

my body to kiss, touch, penetrate or whip, whatever he wishes. Sometimes he likes to punish me a little, it amuses him, as he hates his dependence on me.

Later, when guilt makes him kind, I will satisfy him in one of the many skilful ways I have found it necessary to learn. I am a slim, pale, girly man, with narrow hips and a wiggly walk; my cock is long and thin, my buttocks like two fists. I am in my early forties, perhaps a little older, I am not exactly sure. Because we 'young' don't diddle death beyond fifty, except in exceptional circumstances – if we are brilliant, related to the rich, or sponsored – I have to play my hand soon. I have been planning it for some time. My dream is of my master Raymond, and my mistress Sabine, adopting me. Don't laugh; it's been done by other slaves. I imagine the three of us photographed together on the steps of the government building. Most importantly, I am holding the official papers, and I am safe now, and forever, to age at my leisure – and, importantly, at the leisure of others. My ambition, the ambition of all of us slaves, is to become one of them. To join the old, and take our time to recover from the trauma of being young.

Raymond is wealthy and ancient; we recently celebrated his hundred and fifteenth birthday. He knows well, after I informed him – casually but unforgettably – that one of the major privileges of a man of his wealth and standing will have to be strong, powerful orgasms. Orgasms of an intensity, duration and oceanic plenitude that others are not capable of, the aftershocks of which he could bask in for hours. I convinced him also that his excitement was his spirituality, and that I was drawing the divine through him. What would be the point, after all, of having a business of such a size, run by a huge staff, and with ten properties around the world, if a green-grocer or chauffeur could have your orgasms?

Desire never dies. Like vanity, it can even outlive us. You can try to deny desire; you can try to forget it, or masturbate. But you cannot make love to yourself. And that, as they say, baby, is where I come in.

Raymond is not in great health. He has long, lank, dyed black hair, and a weak neck; when he is tired, his head flops. He has glaucoma, and is losing his sight; full of fluid, his eyes look lazy, the lids drooping. This increases my indispensability, and I am happy to read and write for him. But he still plays bass in his band, and he should live another fifteen years at least; others now are living to a hundred and thirty-five, served by the young like me, who are soon worn out as slaves. The 'old' – those over fifty – have the best healthcare, drugs and prosthetics. They can afford as many professional trainers as they like, but I help my master and mistress work out every day: weights, stretching, running, boxing even.

Outside it is like a Brazilian slum, hot, busy, exhausting, whereas in here there is not a voice to be heard, nor a body to be seen. If you walk the street, contemplating the mad and the frustrated, you soon see how angry everyone is, and how they look like people who have given up too much.

Money buys you space and peace. As a reward for my loyalty, Sabine and Raymond let me use the pool in the house, otherwise it is unused for weeks on end, the lights forever burning over the useless glassy surface. The same applies to the beautiful wood-panelled library, with its unequalled collection. Often I have been the only person working there, developing my mind. But, in the end, like everything else, my mind will always belong to them.

I must admit that I learned with gathering interest and fascination that many great works of literature, for instance *Oedipus*, *Hamlet*, *Karamazov*, are parricidal in nature. Who would not admit that the old must be removed for the young to flourish? A necessary killing is involved here. Otherwise the young will be strapped forever to a rotting corpse.

My question is: suppose the old refuse to get out or move? That is easily conceivable. And suppose they go even further and eliminate those young? Some say that God was never happier than when his son was suffering on the cross, deliriously delighted with the sacrifice of his pathetic offspring even as the boy called out to him. Other sons become suicide bombers out of desperate obedience. I have heard it said that wars have been designed as threshing machines to remove the young.

Here in the land of the old we are caught in this tension. Our fear here is not that people will die, but that they will never die. We will never be rid of them. One day we will have to smash the old bones, those who will not stand out of the way. But this will not be for a long time, and not without real sacrifice and much death.

Raymond and Sabine's generation was considered one of the brightest of all, responsible for a revolutionary, fresh, creative upsurge, in a lucky time when the old was worm-eaten and done for. I learned, in the library, that Raymond, for a time, was a brilliant publicist for his products; he saw, early on, that you are selling yourself, rather than merely a thing. One of his brilliant but simple moves was to use French slogans of resistance and freedom – 'Take your desires for reality'; 'Beneath the street, the beach'; 'It is forbidden to forbid' – and turn them into advertisements for holidays. The simulacrum of freedom was enough for many. He gave them the shadow, not the thing, and how could he not be rewarded for that?

They conquered, his generation, flourishing in the new opportunities of capitalism. Soon after, they closed the roads so no one could follow them up, and now they will not let go. It didn't take them long to see it would be a good idea to enslave the young, whom they patronised, envied and hated, and then, with some exceptions, began to kill off at fifty. For them this was barely murder, but more like abortion, on which they were keen, ridding the world of the not-quite-born and unwanted, of those, they claimed, they could not afford. Those for whom there was no place.

Abandoned by my parents, I came to work for Raymond and Sabine at the age of ten. I was forced to find a decent place in the world by serving them better. When Raymond dictates his poetry to me, which, apparently, is his message, his 'giving back' to the world, I even memorise it, and then I repeat it to him later, with a smile. You will find that the more evil the person, the more likely they are to write poetry. More than this, as a people, you know you're in trouble when your rulers want not only your obedience, but your love.

Sabine is not here today; she prefers to stay in one of the Caribbean properties. I am ageing, and not to everyone's taste, but I taught her to become fond of my charms, and I have learned to overcome my loathing for hers. She is large and lusty, and noisy with it. And when I am done loving her, she likes to be bathed, kissed and talked to. There is nothing so beautiful, or so slow, as watching a woman take a bath. During these conversations I have tried to say to her, 'I want to be your son.'

'But you are my son,' she says, spitting out her champagne. 'And, luckily, not quite my son!'

I have learned that she likes young men between the ages of eighteen and twenty-five to make love to her, and when she doesn't want me, I roam the city looking for beauties, those who know that their only possible advancement lies in serving their elders.

I whine, 'But you must adopt me, mistress, so I can thrive. So I can survive. I know you are becoming bored with me, but I can continue to pick the finest boys for your delectation.'

'I can't see why we should keep you alive,' she chuckles. 'Give me two reasons. No – three, please, these are strait-ened times. I'm sure you know no one can live on just for the sake of it. Everyone has to demonstrate their use, and their ability to care for themselves. The world would collapse if we had billions of elderly people clogging up the hospitals. There can only be a few who will survive. Those who will get through have to be chosen carefully.'

'Why is it always the rich?'

'Because they have done so much to create our stand-ard of living. You know that.'

'Yes, I do.'

Talk about work; I wear myself out keeping Sabine's mood even; she is more bitter and angry than Raymond, who has many other complicated liaisons, being interest-ed in women in general, and even their stories. Having been together for fifteen years, my master and mistress have not one more word to say to one another, except about business. But I continue to spend time with her, improving her love for me. What I did notice, a few years back, is that Sabine has what they call 'everything':

property, jewellery, power, a long life. But she lacks the one thing there really is to want: the fire of love – to be desired passionately. There is no remedy for the disease of desire, except for a rosy mouth on yours, a loving fulfilment, flattery, jokes, and a welcome in the other's eyes. For a long time a boudoir Olivier, I have given her an approximation of that thing, and become a comrade, a companion, even. So, like Jesus, I am also a family therapist, but one who is never allowed to forget that every breath he takes he owes to someone else.

'Where are you, boy? Come on! I wait!'

I hear his voice. Has he been calling for a while? I had become lost in my thoughts. He will be angry. Up I get and hurry towards him. I push the door.

'At last,' he says. 'Where have you been?'

I see, to my surprise, in the corner, a young man washing his hands at the sink. I wonder if he's one of my master's new lovers. If he were, though, he wouldn't be dressed. Raymond always insists on his lovers, whether male or female, attending to him naked since a remarkable and desired body is, these days, of course, an achievement rather than a blessing.

But this man, being younger than me, and with the sort of beauty which could set you dreaming, is clothed. I have to say, without vanity, that he is not unlike a younger version of me. He turns and gives a smooth smile. Then he nods at Raymond.

I am looking at this man, and back at Raymond, when two heavily built guards in uniform enter and take me by the arms. As they lead me away I say, 'Master—'

'Goodbye,' he says, waving. 'However old you are, the truth always comes too late. Goodbye, and thanks.'

A Theft: My Con Man

'Silent, foul spiders spin their web in the base
of our brain . . .'
CHARLES BAUDELAIRE, *Les Fleurs du mal*

I met a man who fed a worm into my ear, and it lived
there for more than a year, where it became comfortable and began to devour my mind and eat into my brain.
Colonised and infected, I was anxious and depressed,
and, at times, a shell. I staggered about like a dying man
and slept as much as I could; being awake was no fun. I
understood hiding, denial and the passion for ignorance.

Sense is usually the last thing that anyone wants to see,
but eventually the truth presses down until you have to
open your eyes. I began to hate this man, whom I had
only recently met, but who had led me on, and then
deceived and stolen from me. At one point, it seemed,
he even pretended to be me. After doing this, he disappeared but rang every day for months, with apologies,
offers of help and mad promises.

I found my hate was so great that not only was it cor-
rupting me – ruining my view of the world until I believed
it was only foul – but, to my surprise, by some mysterious
alchemy, it was turning into love. I was beginning to love

my thief, a man I barely knew, but whom I had trusted and even liked, and who had taken my savings, amongst many other crimes. At one low point I was phoning him every hour. I was impatient with everyone else because I was thinking of him all the time. I was waking up at night to think of him more, and when he did call, my heart leapt. I would retreat to a quiet room where I could hear every tone of his voice. I would, I even thought, go to his house and see him in his privacy. I would become his stalker.

Freud wrote that love involves the undervaluation of reality and the overvaluation of the desired object. While the correct valuation of a person is an odd, if not impossible idea, we might say Freud meant something like this: for various reasons, many of them masochistic, we become involved with others who cannot possibly give what we ask for; we can wait as long as we wish, but they do not have it, and one day, if we can bear to abandon our fantasy and see clearly, we might face reality straight on. We will then look elsewhere for fulfilment, to a place where our needs can, in fact, be satisfied.

At the beginning of this business, one of my agents, the man who had recommended Chandler, had told me how impressive Jeff had been at meetings. Clever and decisive, Chandler had satisfactorily done my agent's accounts, as well as those of my agent's family. Chandler was on top of things. He knew what he was doing.

Everyone felt in good hands. But, by the end, when everything had gone wrong, the truth was that Chandler did not have anything. However, he remained confident and liked to give the impression he did have it all. Or he maintained that he would have it soon: funds were on their way from Spain or Switzerland. And so I kept asking for it, but he knew, and I realised eventually, that he had lost everything. It would never come back, and this was a loss I would have to live with, think about, and attempt to integrate.

*

Pop and the theatre, my first cultural loves, are both, in form and content, games of deception, deceit and mischief, where there is nothing authentic or real behind the artificial front, except the desire to play and to be someone else. David Bowie knew that pop was a put-on; he lifted and modified everything that interested him. I've always been fascinated by the nefarious cleverness of hypnotists, tricksters, card sharps, mountebanks, con men, convincers, deceivers, big-mouths, bigamists, hiders and cheats; men who had three families living in one neighbourhood unbeknownst to one another, others who pretended to be doctors, pilots or Olympic swimmers, or who concealed an evil past as a Nazi. I like to think of the man who tried to sell the Eiffel Tower to an industrialist by convincing him it was to be used for scrap metal.

I think of undercover agents, of anyone who has talked someone into something, someone with nothing who can persuade others, using words, that they have it all, or at least something desirable. The con man is the one who has the password to your hopes, who touches the G-spot of your wishes. Honesty and straightforwardness are dull; the con man makes you aware that life could be more gratifying than it is. He is everyone's procurer, the sorcerer who conjures fantasy in you, the ever-flowing mother who will fill you up with good things, the one who can identify what you want even before you see it yourself. One shouldn't forget that Hans Christian Andersen's tale 'The Emperor's New Clothes' is the story of an almost successful con, of a couple of weavers who convince an Emperor that he is more than he is. His vanity is their instrument, and they play on him until he is exposed and humiliated.

As many of us do, I come from a family of show-offs, fantasists and big-mouths, and I wanted to be big myself, once – bigger than I in fact was. Sometimes I even believed we big-mouths were all in the same game: isn't a writer a kind of con artist or spellbinder, telling stories for their life like Scheherazade, drawing the other into a conspiracy of lies, convincing them to turn the page and believe in flapdoodle?

Naturally, I identified with the con man and his omnipotence over the other, and not with his victims.

But in this case I was the victim; I was the seduced, taken one. Jeff Chandler had helped himself to my money, and he had robbed me of more than that: of an orienting and useful connection with reality, which, once it had slipped away, left me feeling bereft, abject, dizzy and out of control. He had done me over, and done me in.

Long before this, though, and long before I learned that the insane, these days, might disguise themselves as money experts, I had heard that no one had met a sane accountant. Certainly, one of my previous accountants had been unwashed, almost incoherent and, at the end, covered in paint smears, having fallen, he said, into a fence on the way to my place. Nevertheless, before this collapse he'd been a mixture of insanity, probity, cunning and high intelligence.

For my part, I was a good bourgeois bohemian who had always earned a reasonable and steady income. I considered my single duty was to support my children, otherwise I liked not having to think about money. As I needed an accountant, a kind friend then recommended someone competent they knew, but said she sidelined as a rubber-clad dominatrix at night. You could file your expenses and get a whipping. I thanked my friend, but thought that as the work was relatively simple, it might be a good idea to go with the straightest person I could find, a pillar of the community. And Jeff Chandler appeared to be upright. The firm he'd been a partner in for ten years – they'd been around for seventy – were the acme of respectability, with smart offices and a successful clientele. This lower-middle-class clerk would know and follow the rules, so that I could break them in my imagination. That was the idea. What could go wrong?

It was a relief when Jeff turned up at my place, appearing competent, unflustered and on top of it all. What one wants, sometimes, is certainty and a guide, someone who knows better than you what they are doing. Jeff didn't appear to be superinflated like some people. And I'd been trained, as a child, to be something of a truster; as a writer, I was a listener.

*

When the con man walked through my door for the first time, I saw a small, chubby fellow with a high voice whom I could imagine singing enthusiastically in a choir. He wore cheap brown shoes and a clammy suit, and he soon informed me that his hobby was collecting James Bond memorabilia. Alongside his love of thrillers, he managed the finances of several churches, running their fund-raising quiz nights. His Congregationalist church in Essex supported other, similar churches in Albania. This was how, apparently, he had met his Albanian 'fiancée', as he always described the woman he seemed to be involved with. Super-friendly, easy-going with an undogmatic nature, Jeff said I could call anytime. And, indeed, he wore his telephone headphones continuously, muttering away into the mouthpiece even as he walked into my house and sat at my table, waiting for me to fetch him some water. He was always available, he declared, except on Sunday morning, when I was not to ring since he was at church with his family. He was devout, and didn't drink alcohol; he'd never had a hot drink: even the madness of tea had never passed his lips.

He said he took over a hundred phone calls a day. Sometimes he worked for twenty-three hours straight. When busy, he slept only every other day. I thought: well, there's a lot of heroically manic madness about, and most of it is not virulent. Think how agitated fluidity and rushes of ideas can be harnessed, for instance, to art. I liked him; for a while I was fascinated and even envious. Why an artist would envy an accountant might seem a mystery. But doing nothing – a large helping of tedium and dreaming – is essential to a writer's activity. How wonderful to be like him, with such a quick brain, and so in demand. Having so much to do, playing with money so competently, the hours must fly by in a fuss of earthy materialism. In comparison, we artists are of no use at all until others make us so.

Artists are always ambiguous about themselves, and certainly about their position within society. Are we inside or outside? Does what we do have any social utility? Should it have? Are we in showbiz or in service? Just as the dream escapes the utilitarian agency and vigilance of the daily self, and disproves the belief that we can rule ourselves, most proper writers would rather be at what I call the 'Genet' end of the scale, with the criminals, thieves and 'bedlam boys', than situate themselves within the farce and falsity of respectability. Art comes from chaos to make more chaos. The artist escapes the constraint of what he has done before, when he can; he has to. And, every day, I had to struggle against the impulse to become more conventional, to regress to the easy. My fears had been keeping me too safe.

*

The second time Jeff came over he made his move. He told me that the company, as it stated on its website, made investments for its valued clients. Many of his friends, as well as long-term clients, including several other writers (whose names he was not allowed to provide), were investing in a scheme he was running on behalf of the accountancy firm. The idea was to raise two hundred thousand pounds for someone to use as proof of funds. All Jeff had to do was keep my money safely for a hundred and twenty days, before returning it with good interest. He knew I had broken up with my girlfriend, and then with another girlfriend, and had school fees to pay. I was no longer earning a great deal. It was going wrong, my day seemed to be done, and advances for books and films had fallen away for everyone. Interest rates had crashed, and people were losing their jobs. Beneath most of us there is an abyss, and sometimes your foot plunges into it, and you understand something about catastrophe and loss. Most of my contemporaries, the ones who hadn't become rich in the good times, were teaching. The academy had become our patron, as good a use for it as any: we supported the students, and the university bought us time to write.

The interest Jeff offered was high, but that was because it was only a short-term deal, he explained, and I was fortunate to get in on it so late on. More than a hundred and twenty days after my initial investment Chandler paid the interest owed. I left the capital with him, and offered him a larger chunk of money. Muttering into his phone as always, he drove me to the bank to pick it up, his feet barely touching the pedals of his huge 4x4, his computer parked securely on the dashboard.

If he seemed particularly panicky and agitated that day, I put it down to his frantic life. But, looking back, I can see that he knew, at the moment when I signed over the money to him, that he was deceiving me, that it was all a lie, and this money, which I had put aside for my children's education, would be lost. But he said nothing and just smiled. By then I'd given him more than a hundred thousand pounds, which was the money he never returned, the money he stole, either stashing it some-where, or losing it to other scammers.

This, it turned out, was the least of it. During this peri-od, in the spring of 2012, he and I were doing business in a building society not far from my house. Jeff was helping me to 'get more' from my accounts. He asked me to give him my driving licence, which was my ID, to show the assistant at the teller's window. He must have copied it, because a few days later my account at the building soci-ety was empty, having been raided. I didn't become aware of this for a couple of weeks, until I returned to the build-ing society to take out some money and found that my account had been gutted. That moment was like being hit in the face with a brick; I sat down with my head in my hands for some time, attempting to arrange the frag-ments of this story into one piece. I learned, much later, after a lot of confusion, that Jeff had gone into a branch of the building society in North London, where I'd never been, shown some version of my ID, forged my signature and walked out with eighty thousand pounds.

The afternoon of the discovery, despite my shock, some instinct made me continue with my detective work. I went into the branches of several building societies near where I lived, asking if they had accounts in my name. The first two didn't, but it turned out that the third one did. When I enquired about this I had the uncanny expe-rience of being asked by the branch manager if I was 'the real' Hanif Kureishi or an imposter. 'How do we know you're you,' he said, 'and not the other man?' 'I have ID,' I said. 'But he had ID,' he replied.

While I am someone who likes to entertain interesting questions, and never mind the fact the branch manager had become a philosopher of epistemology, I had been taken over. My name belonged to someone else. I had become a nobody, a cipher, while Jeff had turned into me. After ruminating on this vertiginous reversal, I said that an imposter wouldn't be this furious, and wouldn't shout. Surely he would be nervous. 'His signature is the same as yours.' He pushed a copy across the desk. It bore no resemblance to mine. How could I prove that two quite different things were two quite different things? The situation got worse when it turned out that Jeff had also given a false address in South London. I checked the location; it was very near my childhood home. I planned to go there and run into myself, living another life. We could be introduced.

But I hadn't thought this through yet, or even realised Jeff was involved; it hadn't occurred to me. So, after this crime was committed I rang the criminal immediately, knowing he would help me. And he did. Jeff was furious with the building society for handing out my money on a forged signature. He said if he had more time he'd go to the building society and tear a strip off them. It was obvious the signatures wouldn't match. It was like the Wild West out there, he said. There were at least ten thousand fraud attempts a day on British banks, and many of them succeeded. Fortunately, the building society took responsibility – having handed out my money rather easily – and returned the amount. It was a while, though, before I could think this through, and work out that it was Jeff himself who had deceived me, and then attempted to help. I should have gone with Miss Whiplash, the dominatrix.

Also during this period, when Jeff must have been very mad and busy, when the self which had perhaps dominated and contained him seemed to have been overrun by a more sinister invincible self – the whole of his energy and intelligence had become committed to extreme suicidal thievery – Jeff tried to persuade me to raise a mortgage on my house. This would release more funds for his 'investments'. Luckily I didn't proceed, because about a month before Jeff was due to return my capital and the next tranche of interest, I received a phone call from the accountants saying Jeff had been sacked. Another writer had noticed that money was missing from his account, and had warned the firm, who then investigated Jeff's computer. It turned out that Jeff had stolen from the firm in which he was a partner, as well as from numerous other friends, charities and clients whose money he had invested in various flimsy schemes. If I wanted to know what was going on, I should call him – and they gave me his number and email address, and put the phone down. That was the last word his partners said on the matter. Everyone else in the company he worked for denied all responsibility.

It occurred to me to call Jeff. He answered his phone and, as always, he was available and chatty. It was a relief that he hadn't disappeared and was willing to offer an explanation. That evening he came over to my local cafe and told me he'd got into difficulty with the investments. He didn't like the word 'steal', he said, as he'd never intended to keep the money for himself. He had 'moved' people's money about, as financial gaps began to appear around him. He had borrowed money from some clients to pay off others. As he explained this, he also spoke to other clients on his phone; on another phone he was on the internet, on eBay, where he was trying to sell his sofa, some artwork, other household items and, hardest of all, his James Bond toys. His hands were shaking, his voice was weak, he could barely speak.

In Gabriel García Márquez's great story 'There Are No Thieves in This Town' a feckless thief steals the billiard balls from the bar's only billiard table, which is, more or less, the only entertainment in the little flyblown town. As the tale unwraps, we see that this theft causes chaos; there is a tsunami of unintended and unpredictable consequences, of guilt, revenge and violence. By the end the thief is attempting to make reparation, but that also goes wrong. At one point he considers fleeing, as if attempting to get away from himself, so noxious has he become, but where could he go?

It was getting hot for Jeff, recriminations were piling up, and a few days later he fled. He went to Spain, either to hide out from the anger directed his way, or to try to retrieve some of the money which had been stolen from a joint bank account by a lawyer who turned out to be 'a scammer', despite the fact Jeff had had him checked out. It looked as though Jeff had believed he could make some money, but had fallen into a brood of vipers, a nest of crooks. Not that I should worry about anything, he said during one of his daily phone calls from Spain. One of his more trusting investors had given him some money to live on while he recovered the stolen stuff. He was, he told me, right now standing outside the house of the scammer who had stolen our money. He could see the bastard through the window. Jeff had followed and confronted the man when he went to his office. Now the man closed his curtains and didn't go out. Chandler was 'shutting him down'. Jeff had also, undercover, sent hard men to threaten various parties. Not that this Spanish investment was the only one he had going. There was another, in Switzerland, which would come through later. There was no doubt, he said, that the money would turn up. It was only a question of when. What was wrong with a little patience?

He began to call me regularly from Spain, sometimes twice a day. When I told him what anguish and shock this theft, this violation and stupidity, had visited upon me and my family, and when I wondered what the point of his promises was, he'd apologise for what he'd done, saying his only chance was to pay everyone back. There was no point in any of us contacting the police, he said; the money would never be returned if he was in prison. I had to give him one more chance; he knew how to sort it out. Crime hadn't been his career choice, otherwise he'd have disappeared to Albania, where his fiancée's family lived, and where he could, at least, have worked as an accountant. No; he'd made the wrong move because the scheme had looked good to him, and he'd invested for us. And for himself, of course. Still, all would be fine; my money would be returned 'by Thursday'. It became a family joke. He was the 'Thursday man'. Many Thursdays came and went, yet his little squeaky voice was always optimistic. The money would 'definitely' turn up. 'They have no choice,' he'd say. 'It's our money.' It was yes, yes, yes, with him. And so in this way days, weeks, months passed.

Not speaking to the police was the only leverage I had over him. But then he exhorted me to pity him. He had placed himself, I could see, at the centre of a large net-work of people who were dependent on him. Having obtained money from twenty of his friends, as well as members of his own family, all these distressed people were now calling him; they all required information, and he connected us all, sitting in the centre of the shattered mirror of his life, like a broken, helpless king muttering meaningless phrases.

There was another thing. One morning, just before he left for Spain, Jeff had rung to say he hadn't been in contact because his mother's sister had died and he'd been at another funeral. Soon he informed me that two of his investors and three members of his family had recently died. His fiancée's mother was on the verge of death. They were dropping like flies; he seemed to be aware that he was killing everyone around him. We had entered a wild disorder – the realm of death, if not murder – in his mind. But not only had he stolen from me, and, in total, about four million pounds from others, he wanted consolation and support. He had it, too; I threw myself into an orgy of encouragement. What an unlucky fellow he was with everyone dying around him, and what a bad year he was having in this cemetery of ghosts. Was there anything I could do? If he ever needed to talk, I was there. When it occurred to me to go to his house and stand outside, watching his movements and seeing how he lived, I visualised relays of semi-concealed desperate voyeurs observing one another while attempting to remain unnoticed.

Once, later, when I couldn't find him, when his phone

was cut off in Spain because he couldn't pay the bill, I fell into a sort of raging madness, and didn't know what to do with myself. I walked, I punched things and shouted obscenities; at one point, I was phoning him every fifteen minutes. I just had to know where he was. But perhaps he was busy soothing the many others he had reduced to the same condition?

There was nothing sensuous or erotic in all this fury and despair. In fact, it could lead you to believe that life is hopeless, and nothing but a trap. Yet however ridiculous, shaming and humiliating it was, the game could not end. That was the one thing which could not happen. Jeff was the lover I always wanted to hear from and was even keener to see. I would beg him for a 'new lie', and he would give me one, and they were some of the best lies I'd ever heard. He was never haughty, cruel or taunting, but always straightforward, as if he understood that deception was a medicine I required urgently. Forever waiting for my man, I was reminded of a coke dealer I had in the 90s, a sweaty, paranoid madman whose eventual arrival in a knackered Rolls-Royce, with a pit bull – a snuffling violent ball of threat which he would release in my flat – was greeted by me as a great event, as the highlight of the day. I'd given Jeff my savings, why not give him my time and health and life too? Usually, when one believes one is most safe, one is in most danger. But I knew how easy it is to become addicted to catastrophes, and how difficult it is to let go of violent pleasures. What was happening to me?

There's a passage in Nietzsche's *The Gay Science* which states, 'What if a demon crept after you one day and said to you, "This life, as you live it now and have lived it, you will have to live again and again; and there will be nothing new in it, but every pain and every joy and every thought and sigh will have to return to you, all in the same succession and sequence. The eternal hourglass of existence is turned upside down again and again, and you with it, speck of dust."' And in *Thus Spake Zarathustra* Nietzsche writes, 'Time is a circle. Do you desire this innumerable times more?'

I began to wonder if I was being thrust back into something I recognised. I come from a South London suburb, and though Jeff was in his early forties and I'm fifteen years older than him, growing up in 1960s South London I knew plenty of post-war spivs and wide boys like him. The area was full of smart and nasty thieving crooks and off-the-back-of-a-lorry merchants. The other significant interest of the suburban young was music. A lot of bands made the relatively short journey to the suburbs, and many kids were starting to form groups. The music and the drug dealing and thieving had one thing in common, which was a kind of defiance of dead authority and the manufacture of excitement through transgression. But the music we heard and made, and the clothes and creativity which came out of it, was alive, and represented a future, while the thievery was a futility. But I couldn't, then, always tell them apart, and the mad thing was, I still hadn't learned.

*

Chandler told me the police arrested him on the plane when he came back from Spain. This annoyed and embarrassed him in front of the other passengers. 'I wasn't going to run away. They didn't need to do that,' he told me sniffily. Apparently he didn't say much when the police interviewed him, and he was soon on bail. Over Christmas we met a couple of times and he continued to say the money was about to turn up. He was not pleased with the police. They were not giving him the chance to retrieve the money, and they had upset his frail mother by mentioning jail. Couldn't they be more sensitive? I asked him how his Sundays were, how going to church with his family, in such circumstances, made him feel. He said it had been difficult for them all – there had been 'looks' – since it was now known that he had stolen the church fund he had been charged with taking care of. But he was keen to let me know that 'God is a forgiving fellow'.

'That's all right, then,' I said.

'Many of the others will never be repaid, but for you there is still a way out,' he said, leaning forward.

Unsurprisingly for someone so isolated and living in their own mind, there were labyrinths of mysterious complication without conclusion which he confused and bored me with. But it seemed to boil down to this: though he wanted to pay me back, since he'd been pinched by the police and couldn't move money around in his own name, I had to open an account in Nevada or the Channel Islands. That way the money wouldn't show up in my bank statements. Or I could, he said, go to Switzerland, pick up the money in cash, and carry it in a suitcase to another bank. I pictured myself walking around Geneva with thousands of euros in a bag, and while the idea made me laugh, I wondered how things had come to such a pass, and what my children would think. I told him I was ready to book my flight. I was keen to see Geneva, even in winter.

In the cafe that day, examining this peculiar little Lucifer in his cheap shoes, as his phones buzzed at his fingertips, a man who had just smugly announced he'd forgiven himself, I considered the enigma of madness. How could he appear so unworried? How could he deem a catastrophe and the creation of so much fury a local difficulty? I wanted to know him, but he did not want to know himself. Nothing about his own state of mind concerned him. Perhaps his actions were his only thoughts, and there was nothing in his mind at all. Not that distress did not exist. He had inserted it into us, his victims, rendering us afraid, depressed, furious, sleepless, guilty, while he was blithe and even jaunty. Not that such separation doesn't happen all the time. In this Hollywood world of heroes and villains, good and evil are kept apart; there is no confusion, ambiguity or subtlety. And when, at the end of the Hollywood piece, the two antitheses confront one another and fight to the death, good always succeeds. But when evil is a form of goodness, when, say, it is innocent or even altruistic, there occurs something which cannot be grasped, let's call it an impossibility. And it was this I was trying to know, and, eventually, write from or out of.

Jeff told me he was ringing his victims regularly, to calm them down and keep them informed, though one of his school friends, whom he persuaded to invest his savings, was about to lose his house. But still I wouldn't hear it when people I'd confided in dismissed Jeff as a toxic little thief. Jeff was a hero for wanting to make reparation; he was doing his best: he was aware he had almost run out of chances. If idiots are elevated into gods all the time, he was at least my idiot. Not only were we friends, I would continue to believe that he would deliver me into the light, and then I would be happy and free. Yet how is it that people can get stuck inside you, like dreams which refuse to yield up the secrets of their horror, and you can't wake up or grasp what's going on? I began to mirror his behaviour. Manically obsessed with him, I couldn't sleep. I wished him to die, but ended up wishing I could die.

*

As I walked about, thinking him through, it came back to me, after a while, where I had seen something like this before. Had Jeff always been there? In what sense had he – or a man resembling him – always been present in my life? And when I wasn't using him to undermine and depress me, what use could he be? Would I have to look at his face forever? For there were, when I could bear to think about it, an eternity of Jeffs, of mostly older men whose stories I'd attend to. There are friends you begin to hate even as you love them, even as they waste you, and you refuse to see how tiresome and what an expense it all is. What emerges in such friendships is the same thing repeatedly, until both partners become sadistic. The ending of significant friendships is painful, yet still I believe in the future; rebirths are possible: there are conversations where new things can be said and heard.

*

My father, born in Madras, had been at the younger end of a large family of mainly boys who were rough and competitive. In his early twenties my father came from Bombay to London to study and to make a new life. He married an Englishwoman, left college and settled in the suburbs, where the quiet and regularity suited him, and he liked the people. But Dad's job, in the Pakistani

Embassy, was dull and badly paid, and without a pension. My mother and I urged him to find a better job and, at one point, he considered joining the police as a clerk. He also considered becoming a traffic warden. But in the end Dad refused to change. He thought he was better than all that: another job was unimportant, it was nothing, because soon, he imagined, he'd become a writer. He would have the dignity and class an artist deserved. But until then we had to provide encouragement and support, keeping the faith. We were supposed to be fans and believers, maintaining the master in his place. Our love and confidence would keep him afloat, just as the prayers of the faithful keep God from discouragement. Whatever happened, we could never be disappointed in Dad; the good thing would turn up. After all, self-belief is necessary, isn't it? And, surely, one should have grit and never give up.

However, I figured out, years later, that I in particular had been persuaded. I had betrayed a more thoughtful and realistic position, getting everything the wrong way round. Somehow I had joined a protection racket or cult. Whatever happened, Dad couldn't be disenchanted, or taste the bitterness of failure. It had become my job, as his disciple and imitator, to shield him from truths which, however tough they might have been, could have made him more imaginative. That was my naivety; but I was young, and this was ages ago, before I could recognise how necessary and important disappointment is, and long before I saw that others' delusions keep them sane, but don't necessarily do the same for us.

*

In many other ways, my mates and cohorts and those a bit older in the 60s and 70s, mature property owners now, were a generation of hoodwinked fools. We, who had denounced and given up on numerous authorities, had sought new masters over and over again. Friends, and those in our circles, were Maoists, Stalinists and Trotskyites of various types; others I knew followed Scientology and similar groups, like EST (Erhard Seminars Training), to which they showed cult-like dedication. We doubters seem to be easily impressed by those with conviction. And it is the attitude of the believer rather than the belief itself which is the crucial thing here. Whether it's political or scientific salvation, seventy-two virgins waiting in heaven, a particular example of satanic ritual abuse, or the idea that one has a crucial message of liberation for the world, it is the state of absolute certainty and dogmatism which is the menace. The idea that by removing the object of the delusion one will cure the delusion is itself a delusion. Delusions are two-a-penny; what is significant is the attitude taken towards the material. Any fool can believe the sun will rise tomorrow: it takes a certain kind of absurd commitment to believe in, say, the efficacy of lifelong celibacy, or prayer or heaven, or some kind of political paradise – or to believe in a con man. It is the absurdity of the belief which makes the commitment to it absolutely necessary, and the intractability of the conviction will be in inverse proportion to the unsustainability of the idea.

In my case absurdity had certainly created commitment. I and some others kept Jeff going, as if he had started his own religion. But it was from this engagement with Jeff that a question formed in my mind, one of the most important there is. Can one person drive another person mad, persuading them to forsake that which is truly of value, collapsing their mind so they see reality askew? Certainly, adults can drive children mad, and adults can make one another crazy by creating conflicts in them which seem insoluble, or for which the only solution might appear to be a retreat into inner chaos and disintegration. Jeff seemed to have that effect on me. But if my head was parked under the bed, I had to wonder about my own part in putting it there. I seemed to have willingly joined a sect and come to believe that my suffering was worthwhile and would lead, eventually, to relief and happiness. I had believed Jeff was the solution when he was the problem, and that my madness was the only thing keeping me sane.

Sometimes you can only get anywhere by giving up on people, by cutting the links between you. How do you begin to do that? With Jeff, it felt as if he was no longer a real person in the world, but, rather, as if I'd swallowed but could not digest him. People can kill themselves to get rid of a devilish persecutor inside them.

*

The last time we met, in a cafe near my house, Jeff wasn't in good shape. His fiancée seemed to have disappeared, and she didn't want to know anything about where he'd got so much money from, or even hear from him again. Thugs had been coming to his place to threaten him, and he'd had to call the police. It seemed to me that his mania had surrendered to disintegration; his body had given up and he couldn't get out of bed or wake up properly. He could barely breathe or talk. I told him that it had been nine months since my money had gone missing, and I was going to give a statement to the police. He looked alarmed and promised to give me a 'little bit' on Monday, and he winked. To prove it – and, perhaps to keep up appearances – he showed me a bank statement for forty-three million rials belonging to a Dubai sheik he'd 'invested' for.

I laughed and attempted to add to the bitterness of his woes by telling him that I'd worked briefly in a women's prison and could still recall the hopeless cries of the self-harmers and the clink of keys being turned in locks. He nodded and said that it was now inevitable that he would have to do 'time'. He knew he wouldn't like it in jail, particularly as he was claustrophobic. His voice began to break, and he said he'd only stolen money – or 'borrowed' it, as he preferred to put it – when he'd received a notice claiming to deliver £350,000 to his account. He'd then begun to move money around, and everything went crazy, as it can when you get desperate and start to panic. I visualised him being encircled by those he'd wanted to enrich; and I knew he feared being shut in, and returned to the place he was most afraid of. The claustrophobic desires his own immurement, and he had brought it about that he would be shut in for a long time.

That's justice for you, and as I watched the sexless, bland bean counter walk away, it just seemed obvious that time is more valuable than money. It took me a while to see this. Chandler had done me a terrible disservice by creating the impression that money was the only important thing in the world, that it was love itself, the milk of paradise, the medium that mattered the most, being more important than ideas, or poetry, or friendship or conversation. This was the point at which communism and capitalism met: where the single value was the crudest form of social utility.

*

One day I was released – by the pitying look on a good friend's face. After he'd heard me out for at least the third time, he was firm. 'More than enough already,' he said. 'This has gone too far. Let him go.'

'Has it gone too far? Are you sure?'

'All you can do is write it out.'

My heart sank, and my instinct was to resist such a terrible truth, one which was disruptive and uncomfortably liberating, connecting me to that which Henry James referred to as 'the grim face of reality'. After all, the masochistic bond is one of the strongest there is. We choose our oppressors; we love them like our parents. Doesn't La Boétie write somewhere, 'Freedom is the one thing which men have no desire for'? I wandered around for a few days as if I'd been punched. Eventually, I dragged myself to my desk. Perhaps my friend was correct; perhaps there was nothing else for it but the breaking of that bond of voluntary servitude, and serious reflection. Jeff had enlarged my fears, at times making them very large indeed. But at least I could see what they were. I had to find a way to live around them.

It is exhausting work to disperse all goodness and create futility and pointlessness. None of this wild fantasy had been good for Jeff, for me, for anyone. Artists have an imagination, their minds can go anywhere, but their feet have to be on the ground, and their words organised. Insofar as it was possible, I would have to see Jeff as he was, and consider what I'd made of him. It can be real work keeping alive the most important things, and everybody hides from that which matters most to them. When it comes to writing, it is probably true that human weakness in all its varieties is the only subject there is, and I had had more than enough of that.

I began to write, throwing down thoughts as they occurred to me, while not being sure as I began on this piece that writing is quite the cure it can be made out to be. Not only is writing an indirect and long-term form of communication, but doesn't writing open a wound before it heals it?

However: alone you cannot achieve anything; alone you can only return to where you were as a child. Writing is an adult transaction; there is always someone there, a real target, as it were, for your words, which should be open-ended and fresh. Words are the strongest material there is, and telling stories is a form of action which changes reality. My relationship with Jeff was not dead; it was worse than that, it had been actively destructive and still was, its only consolation and reward being a little perverse excitement and complicity. For me to try and find another way through this difficulty was to give up my addiction to the idea that he would deliver. Loss is the price of knowledge: I would have to forsake something comparatively easy for something more difficult, forfeiting the accelerations of love and hate for the relatively low mood of mere sadness and acceptance. Art, like the best conversation, re-frames conflicts, representing them in ways which enable fresh thought, generating more plausible stories. A third thing, something brand new, would eventually have to emerge from the stasis and despair of this filthy, stupid dialectic. After all, I wondered, who did my mind belong to – my father, my children, my accountant? How could I retrieve it? What agency did I have over it? It seemed to me, after all this, that having a peaceful, creative mind was a most desirable thing. The most fortunate people, it seemed, were those with least anxiety, and I was a long way from that.

The police had written to me about Jeff. While I'd been giving Jeff a chance to come up with the money, I hadn't replied. Now, after my hopes had run their vain course, I called them. They were well aware of Jeff, and had been gathering material and information. However, several victims hadn't been found or come forward. Some were too rich to notice or get embroiled. Many of these suckers were understandably embarrassed; they'd been greedy and seduced, and couldn't admit to themselves or their families what they had let Jeff do to them. Some believed they had insufficient evidence to prosecute him, and others were still helping Chandler, chained to the illusion, believing he would deliver, unable to give up on him.

In the early spring of 2013, about a year after Jeff had gone on his spree, a detective came to take a statement from me. The policeman had recently been to see Jeff, who lived in a grim bungalow out in semi-rural Essex, with his parents in a shabby place at the other end of the plot of land. The policeman called it a backward, churchy, semi-rural community, with very little worth selling. Greed was always understandable, he said, but Chandler's behaviour was inexplicable. This man was doing well; he had come far for someone with his background. As a partner in his accountancy firm, his already large income would only increase. Why would he sabotage himself for a relatively small amount of dodgy money?

The policeman said Jeff seemed naive. A lot of people said that about him. He must have been led on by the Albanian girl he called his fiancée, and they had spent six or seven thousand pounds in one weekend at the Westfield shopping centre. Jeff had bought property in Albania, a hairdressing salon, a bakery and a restaurant, and put them in her name. Jeff had once been quick and smart, and a lot of people had told him that. But there is always a horizon to people's intelligence, and they must bear that in mind, since it is their fate. But Jeff, with his James Bond omnipotence, couldn't do that. There were no limits in the con man's world, and perhaps he had come to believe he could do just anything, steal and steal, and yet feel free. However, where there is no prohibition there is no meaning, and nothing real is possible. You would, I suppose, begin to feel megalomaniacal and unconnected. In truth, Jeff was ultimately a self-deceiver, a seducer who had seduced himself, and a taker who had also been taken.

When the truth was discovered, Jeff's colleagues and former friends, people who had worked with him for more than ten years, some of whom he had employed and many of whom he stole from, scattered and scurried away. Bewildered and devastated by his deception, by all they did not know, they denied any responsibility for this disaster. They had not noticed he was a madman. Hiding behind lawyers gives people a sort of agency, or symbolic power, but it also exposes how weak they are. They're like people wearing a fright mask, and when it is ripped off you see the awful human fear beneath.

What shocks about a crime, I noticed, is not only the violation of limits, but the new knowledge of how insubstantial those limits were in the first place. Why, then, is it a relief and a disappointment when it turns out that the authorities, those we leaned against and even believed in, are themselves – and always were – foolish, perverse and dishonest?

*

Far from being an exception, a good man who inexplicably went wrong, Jeff was a monster created by the accountancy firm he partly built. As the necessary excrescence of the system, he embodied the Thatcherite ideal perfectly. Lower middle class, religious, a family man, self-motivated and hard working, he loved money more than he loved himself; he was a chancer, a corrupted wide boy, a charming crook who not only rose to the top of his profession, but destroyed everything around him. In the end, of course, the manic swings and crashes of bipolar capitalism had taken him too, but at least I understood now that far from being a maverick, an exception, the con man, the thief and liar, the man with the over-the-top interest rate, was the money world's most representative figure. A lunatic at the centre of a corrupt, collapsing system, like the 'mad' child in a family, he was its essence, the symptom that spoke its truth.

This view might be right. But it might not be. It is a good, convincing story, and anyone would rightly be suspicious of such cohesion and all that it excludes. So, such a narrative is probably irrelevant. But I couldn't stop thinking about Jeff and what sort of person he might be. Because he was no Machiavelli, plotting for advantage, power or wealth; he wasn't focused, predictable or readable. It must be odd to have nothing about you that is true, so I wanted to know what it would be like to be false through and through, a man you could look at and see nothing. I had, eventually, spoken to friends in the press about this story and some of it had become public, though the behaviour of Jeff's partners in the company had become disconcerting. However, I stuck to this thought: my money might have been stolen, but my words couldn't be. Yet even after this, and after he'd been arrested but not charged, I heard that Jeff was still peddling investments and spinning stories, a mad novelist, and a far-out magic realist at that, who couldn't stop making it up. I tried to get in touch with him, to ask him what he thought he was doing. He wouldn't answer. Jeff was not a great Dostoevskian criminal or poet of destruction, he was not truly selfish or savage when it came to the violation of limits. There was no additional liberty in his impotent transgressions; the rules were still in place. What he did was a form of random evil in its most banal sense, but he did become good at it, successfully causing despair, hopelessness and ruin. Not everyone can bear to do that; not everyone would want to face the consequences, to reap such hatred. But Jeff lacked imagination, taking no one anywhere. He was a destructive monster, and he was nothing of interest.

*

Though a lot of people lost important things, this was only a minor tragedy. But it made people who heard about it nervous. They saw that anyone could be found out and taken, however defended they might be, because everyone is dependent on someone else, and there is always something unknowable about others. However, I was duped by a con man but learned more about women than I'd known before. Women were outraged by the wrongness; the women came through, and taught me to depend on them. You can be direct with a woman and she will appreciate it. The women rang the appropriate people; they wrote letters, they talked to one another, and knew what to do. They blamed the right people.

It is no surprise that we are all spellbound by crime and criminality. As children we are continuously taught right and wrong and morality; we are exhorted to obedience and are tempted by defiance. We are told that if we behave well we will be rewarded, but we soon notice that these rewards mostly benefit the authority rather than us. At the same time, we sexualise disobedience and never abandon its dangerous compulsions. This makes it more difficult, rather than easier, to be free. For adults, most of television, cinema, the newspapers and fiction is concerned with detectives, offenders and punishment. And for good reason. This is where we think about whether we should be good or not, and what the cost of crossing the line is, and what the – usually higher – cost of renunciation is. This is where we think about the relation between pleasure and happiness, and between pleasure and its price. After all, most authorities are experts in denial. Where might we learn what pleasure really is, and who will teach us?

*

Jeff's fiancée, or his desire for her, might have been the detonator, but Jeff himself had become a little suicide bomb, devastating everyone around him. It turned out that Jeff stole from his friends – people he'd known since he was eleven – from the church his parents attended, from charities, writers, pension funds, and of course from his partners at the company he had helped build. The line he gave the victims, and the stories he told, his circuitous explanations, as the whole thing broke down were all the same. Painful conflicts between friends and colleagues broke out after Jeff's crimes. People argued, let one another down, and fell out. I yelled at people until I had to lie down. Jeff taught me, I guess, the necessity of boldness and exactitude in speech. Where before I'd been evasive and vague, I had to learn to be precise, and ask for what I needed. Then, once this story came out in the press, many people wrote to me and to each other. Some could only get in contact anonymously, and many chose to be ashamed. People believed that because they had fantasised about becoming richer they had actively collaborated in their own downfall. It was as if, for this minor crime of greed, each person had been seduced, fucked, fucked over, and discarded. However, some of the victims continued to defend Jeff, calling him 'innocent' or 'naive'. Of course, it was this facade of naivety which made him so dangerous and convincing. But there was also a part of him which was genuinely naive. It might have been the case that his sexual inexperience had made him hazardous, because he hadn't understood what was happening to him when he met the Albanian woman. He thought he had to impress her. Or give her everything. I remember now that the first time I met him he opened his wallet in order to show me a photograph of the woman he called his fiancée. The picture was indistinct but I could see that it was, at least, a woman. This action seemed an incongruous, old-fashioned thing to do. I thought he was showing me that the successful man is one who is loved. Now I know it was the wallet, not the woman, he wanted me to see.

*

Thieves of time, thieves of friendship, affection and sexuality, thieves of your soul, stealers of dreams: bad loves, and even worse loves. The obscene, perverse, sadomasochistic death dance, both partners locked together in limbo. You could call these anti-loves. People love their suffering, and most thefts are even welcomed, as you can barely wait to give away that which is most valuable; and there are many thefts you don't notice because you are paying attention to the wrong things. When you do see at last, it can be a shock. Twilight: time is running down; there has to be an attempt at reparation – a release, if not a rebirth, converting action into thought and renewed creativity, into a better madness. Ruthlessness, particularly with oneself, is an art.

I know I'm ready for something fresh when I want to buy new notebooks. With scores of new pages to fill and flip through in anticipation, I can begin to believe I'm a writer again, the void of the empty page being an invitation and a limit to the disorder of my ideas.

My talent, such as it is, had not yet deserted me. Whether I was distracted or not, I could write; I liked to write and worked longer hours than before. I like to wake up in the morning with the whole day ahead of me, in which I can write uninterruptedly. My writing was developing and changing, even if other things were getting worse by staying the same. I began to scribble these notes, and wonder about what sort of thief an artist is. Things had got too predictable in my life, and unpredictability – at least in the head – is the engine of creativity. I knew that I needed more imagination here. To be liberated from someone is to no longer have the enervating burden of thinking of them: that is one lesson that love can teach. How long had it been since I'd gone a day without this fool flailing in my mind? He had made me into someone I didn't like, and for a time I hated to wake up to myself. Jeff had taken my money, but what else had he taken? He had come far, according to the policeman, but I had come further, and would go much further. To be happy, I had to forget, and that is difficult.

I thought: I should steal from him. If I stole something back from this devil and homunculus, I could transform and remake him, pinning him to the page. If my despair had made me wonder what art might be for, I could at least now see that art is a glorious binding Eros, making new unities. Art might seem mad at times, but it has boundaries and structure; it has to. Where there was nothing there would be something new, a moment of light, an upsurge, invention. As an artist you have to force yourself to turn and look at the world, and the world is always worse, and more interesting, than you can imagine or render.

Credits

'Anarchy and the Imagination' (as 'What they don't teach you at creative writing school'): *Daily Telegraph* (2014); 'The Racer': *New Statesman* (2013); 'His Father's Excrement: Franz Kafka and the Power of the Insect': *Critical Quarterly* (2014); 'The Art of Distraction': *New York Times* and *The Times* (2012); 'Weekends and Forevers' (as 'In praise of adultery'): *Guardian* (2013); 'This Door Is Shut': *Red – Waterstones' Inaugural Anthology* (2012); 'These Mysterious Strangers: The New Story of the Immigrant' (as 'The migrant has no face, status or story'): *Guardian* (2014); 'We Are the Wide-Eyed Piccaninnies' (as 'Knock, Knock, it's Enoch') *Guardian*, (2014).

Also by Hanif Kureishi

The Last Word

Shortlisted for the Bollinger Everyman Wodehouse Prize

Mamoon is an eminent Indian-born writer who has made a career in England – but now, in his early seventies, his reputation is fading, his book sales have dried up and his new wife has expensive tastes. Harry, a young writer, is commissioned to write a biography to revitalise Mamoon's career. He greatly admires Mamoon's work and wants to uncover the truth of the artist's life, but Harry's publisher seeks a more salacious tale of sex and scandal to generate headlines. Meanwhile, Mamoon himself is mining a different vein of truth altogether – but which one of them will have the last word?

'Kureishi's best work to date – it is very funny.' *The Times*

'Kureishi at his mischievous, subversive best.' *Independent* Book of the Week

'Brilliantly funny and entertaining.' *Evening Standard*

ff

Something to Tell You

Jamal Khan, a psychoanalyst in his fifties living in London, is haunted by memories of his teens: his first love, Ajita; the exhilaration of sex, drugs and politics; and a brutal act of violence which changed his life for ever. As he and his best friend Henry attempt to make the sometimes painful, sometimes comic transition to their divorced middle age, balancing the conflicts of desire and dignity, Jamal's teenage traumas make a shocking reappearance in his present life.

'Superb . . . No one else casts such a shrewd and gimlet eye on contemporary life.' William Boyd

'A great comic writer, and a peerless connoisseur of the human mystery.' *Independent*

'A novel that describes with such elegant seriousness the fear of ageing, the inanition of pleasure, the survival of love, the longing to understand and be understood.' *Sunday Telegraph*

ff

The Buddha of Suburbia

Winner of the Whitbread First Novel Award

The hero of Hanif Kureishi's first novel is Karim, a dreamy teenager, desperate to escape suburban South London and experience the forbidden fruits which the 1970s seem to offer. When the unlikely opportunity of a life in the theatre announces itself, Karim starts to win the sort of attention he has been craving – albeit with some rude and raucous results.

'Utterly irreverent and wildly improper, but also genuinely touching and truthful. And very funny indeed.' Salman Rushdie

'A wonderful novel. I doubt I will read a funnier one, or one with more heart, this year, possibly this decade.' Angela Carter, *Guardian*

'One of the best comic novels of growing up, and one of the sharpest satires on race relations in this country that I've ever read.' *Independent*

ff

The Black Album

Shahid, a clean-cut young man from the provinces, comes to London after the death of his father. In the capital he falls in love with Deedee Osgood, a college lecturer, and finds himself passionately embroiled in a spiritual battle between liberalism and fundamentalism. *The Black Album* is set in the London of 1989, the year after the second summer of love and the year the infamous fatwah was imposed on Salman Rushdie. It is a thriller for the rave generation by one of the most praised and influential writers of the times.

'Marvellous . . . Kureishi's panoramic London is noisily exuberant.' *Sunday Times*

'*The Black Album* is British Literature. While Kureishi mocks that literature and its milieu, loves it, rejects it and annoys it, novels like *The Black Album* are also transforming it.' *The Times*

ff

Intimacy

'It is the saddest night, for I am leaving and not coming back.' So begins Jay in Hanif Kureishi's coruscating story of the end of a relationship.

'It is by far the most astute and painful dissection of male sexual restlessness that I've read . . . The dialogue is shattering and there's a blunt refusal to compromise or to be fastidious . . . Telling the truth is always a precarious business, but Kureishi does it with seriousness, tenderness and upsetting aplomb.' *Mail on Sunday*

'If, as John Updike says, the duty of a writer is to deliver what he thinks is true, then Kureishi has succeeded: the honesty here is excoriating.' *Observer*

'*Intimacy* speaks to, and for, a lost generation of men: those shaped by the Sixties, disorientated by the Eighties and bereft of a personal and political map in the Nineties.' *Independent on Sunday*

ff

The Body

The centrepiece of Hanif Kureishi's volume of fiction is 'The Body', in which an ageing playwright accepts a tempting offer to have his mind transplanted into a younger physique, but must then face the dire consequences of this decision to chase after his vanished youth.

'*The Body* is written with Kureishi's usual brevity and cool precision. The effect of reading him is cumulative: you are impressed by a certain intensity, and indeed integrity, of vision.' *Observer*

'There is no British writer more adept at articulating the impulses and latent regrets that frame a man's life.' *GQ*

'Kureishi's insights into the human condition remain as accurate and important as ever. Love, parenthood and the problem of happiness are subjects on which he writes with a rare warmth and humanity . . . Some of the most affecting and beautiful prose to be published this year.' *Daily Mail*

ff

Gabriel's Gift

The protagonist of Hanif Kureishi's delightful novel is Gabriel, a fifteen-year-old North London schoolboy trying to come to terms with a new life, after the equilibrium of his family home has been shattered by the ousting of his father. Fending for himself, as well as providing emotional support to his confused (and confusing) parents, Gabriel is forced to grow up quickly. The only support he can draw upon is from his remembered twin brother, Archie, and from his own 'gift', which is accompanied by sensations that urge him into areas of life requiring the utmost courage and faith. A chance visit to seventies rock star Lester Jones crystallizes the turbulent emotions inside Gabriel, and helps him recognise and engage with his gift . . .

'Hugely engaging . . . Kureishi fashions his narrative with wit and immense charm.' *Independent*

'*Gabriel's Gift*, sketched in pastels, returns to the Kureishi of sweet sarcasm and affectionate banter . . . A charming, light-textured fable about talent, about how single-minded creativity might embrace and even by buoyed by the heartbreaking muddle of everyday life.' *Observer*

ff

Midnight All Day

In this astonishing collection of stories, Hanif Kureishi confirms his reputation as Britain's foremost chronicler of the loveless, the lost and the dispossessed. The characters in *Midnight All Day* are familiar to all of us: frustrated and intoxicated, melancholic and sensitive, yet capable of great cruelty, and, if necessary, willing to break the constraints of an old life to make way for the new.

'Each book has been better than the last, and this is no exception . . . The writing in this book is sparer than in his earlier work, with cracking dialogue.' *Daily Telegraph*

'Kureishi creates fiction which although narrow in focus, is powerful and true, leavened by a sharp wit that rarely deserts him.' *The Times*

'For a writer with a fine track record in comedy, Kureishi is a master of the elegiac. He can convey, with enviable simplicity, the pain of lovers mourning past glories.' *Sunday Telegraph*

ff

Love in a Blue Time

Hanif Kureishi's subject is the painful and serious business of love, and its dark flip-side, hate. Like his celebrated novels, these stories are funny, inventive, sexually frank and aggressively contemporary. The characters that arise from these pages – however damaged, deranged or even despicable they may be – are united by one common trait: they are all creatures driven by strong desires.

'A highly enjoyable and elegant collection.' *The Times*

'There is, in the tender honesty of his writing and in his understanding of the mercurial nature of our lives, a rare beauty.' *Daily Mail*

'Kureishi's eye for the zeitgeist is as strong as ever . . . The result is prose that has immense immediacy.' *Independent*

ff

Collected Stories

The short fiction – collected here for the first time – of one of Britain's most acclaimed contemporary writers.

The stories in this collection are, by turns, provocative, erotic, tender, funny and charming, dealing with the complexities of relationships as well as the joys of children. This volume contains Hanif Kureishi's controversial 'Weddings and Beheadings', the prophetic 'My Son the Fanatic', about the religious tensions within the Muslim family, as well as eight new stories.

'The stories in this outstanding collection are to be read not once, but many times.' Helen Dunmore, *The Times*

'Suffused with the author's brazen eroticism and his dark wit . . . this anthology suggests that Kureishi's short stories might be his best work.' *TLS*

'The book's sustained immersion in middle-aged misery is scarily convincing [and] his handling of the form is appealingly non-reverent.' *Guardian*